SPECIAL WELFARE
WELFARE
·
SOCIAL
WARFARE

SPECIAL WELFARE

·

SOCIAL WARFARE

ADOLESCENCE TO ADULTHOOD —
A GUIDEBOOK

THOMAS J. LAGRAVE JR.

Publisher
Honor Bound Academy Books

Copyright © 2024 by Thomas J. LaGrave Jr.

Cover Designer Chelsea McKenna Design
Book Interior Designer Happenstance Type-O-Rama
Reference Citations Barbara McFarland
Editor Andrea Hall
Photographer Michelle Feileacan Photography
Production Manager Kerry Rego

ISBN number 979-8-9906647-0-8 (print)
ISBN number 979-8-9906647-2-2 (epub)

Printed in United States

Dedicated to:

The pursuit of defining yourself,
to knowing yourself. Understanding that it is not what you
do, it is what you are that is important.

In homage to the Vietnam era SEALs who instructed me,
you taught attention is never sought, deeds never shared,
and the most successful OP the one that leaves no trace.
I now embrace the myths, mysteries, and magic combined
with your teachings to begin a final journey....

For me, in retrospect,
I am Adolescent Combat Diplomate.

CONTENTS

PROLOGUE

"... the fate of empires depends upon the education of youth."

—ARISTOTLE

I've written this book to tell you a story, share with you the design of an innovative program with summary and financials in hope that you, dear readers, will invest financially in this very important social support program and stay connected to me via email as I provide actionable solutions to you and your loved ones.

All too often, we awaken to another day of uneasy feelings, bordering on dread. Could it be those feelings are with us because of a question left unanswered? Such as, *"What's really going on?"* Or, perhaps it is due to a deception apropos, the truth? Regardless, what we wake up to each morning appears, as I see it, to be a plethora of inaccurate truths, those that do not form an absolute truth, but instead a fabricated truth, one that causes us to pause, to hesitate, to feel uneasy as if time is running out. Here is where I make my stand, having for years immersed myself in the ways of adolescence. In the pages to follow I offer you insight, clarity, and conviction meant to awakening the strength in you that comes from being born free.

Chapter One

A GIFT GIVEN

The long-awaited day has finally arrived—it's high school graduation day. For the past year, you've been your school's senior class, you are the elder statesmen and stateswomen. You're eighteen and about to embark upon the greatest journey of your life. Parents, teachers, coaches, and friends have prepared you for this moment for nearly two decades. You are talented, capable, competent, and fearless. Nothing can stand in the way of your dreams. Now, the greatest challenge you'll ever face is upon you— adulthood. For this effort you possess all the knowledge you need for your future, or do you? It is obvious you're ready for success, but are you prepared for failure? I would like to offer each of you a gift, the very same gift I was given long ago from a group of teenagers just like you. The wonderful gift they offered me was true friendship and all that it entails. They offered it in the form of unconditional love, and now I offer it to you in the same way—with unconditional love.

That gift was given to me at a time when I had lost everything. Friends wanted nothing to do with me, family had changed the locks on all their doors, and the world, as I saw it, was a cold, lonely place.

After such an introduction, can I hope that you'd be interested in my gift of unconditional love? The reason I'm going to try is because of the world I now see. Never, in all my years, have I felt as I do currently.

We as a nation are coming to a crossroads, a time when the division amongst us may betray all we hold sacred.

This gift of true friendship may appear as though I am offering it only to the youth of this country. Not so, this gift is intended for everyone. Am I being Facetious? Perhaps. Nonetheless, in the following pages, I will share a story in the form of a soliloquy. Using this format we'll explore the question, "What's really going on in our nation?" I will present certain facts that I have researched, written, and believe to be true. I'll share who I am, what I am, and what the point of this endeavor—this gift, is all about. Most importantly, I will offer a suggestion of how we can bring about change—a change that may alter many of the divisions that plague us. By providing knowledge and information specifically for our youth, I believe can profoundly improve their well-being, and benefit all in our society.

In friendship, the gift begins with understanding the circumstances of a worst-case scenario. When it comes to accomplishing an important goal, such as entering adulthood, this must always be considered. At the beginning of any endeavor, you hope for the best but plan for the worst. Personally, after many tumultuous years, embracing this lesson has proven invaluable. It has led me to this point, where presently I'm faced with a challenging goal along with a worst-case scenario, which has manifested as an impregnable wall. This particular wall represents a dark destructive future if not properly addressed. When this type of situation happens, there are usually only two options: quit or find another way.

In order to make this clear, I'll share with you a past memory of similar circumstance, related to a previous personal goal, along with its worst-case scenario. The stage is set, we find ourselves transported to a room in the Welsh highlands of the United Kingdom. This room is located on the top floor of a bed and breakfast. Outside the window and below, there is an ancient stone bridge. A torrent of water flows over the falls, under the bridge, and past my window on its journey toward the sea. I was sitting there because I wished to be surrounded by ancient man-made history and nature's ancient power. This type of environment always helps me attain clarity and focus as I seek answers to elusive problems. During this time I'd been directed to several other unique rooms. Over the past five years, my job title has been Military and Family Life Counselor, "MFLC" for short. Where I'm embedded specifically with Special Operations Command (SOCOM), working alongside Special Forces, including Navy SEALs, Army Rangers, Night Stalkers, Green Berets, Marine Raiders, Air Force Combat Controllers, PJs, and Special Reconnaissance (SR) personnel.

Being surrounded by these quiet professionals creates a unique environment. Through my work with our military's elite warrior's, in large part is why giving up on the important goal I spoke of, was not an option. Finding a way to overcome the impossible is the only option. Confused! When it comes to telling a story, especially this one, it's difficult to understand when you start in the middle of it. For the greatest effect, it is best to start at the beginning, this way it tends to make better sense in the end. Going back to the start of this particular story, or memory, I am nineteen years old. Location, the Silver Strand in Coronado, California. The desire for this magnificent goal, to graduate from Basic Underwater Demolition/SEAL (BUD/S) training and then become a Special Forces Operator. On the Ocean side of the Naval Amphibious Base, is a compound located on the Strand. In one corner of that compound is a bell. During training the easiest thing to accomplish at BUD/S is for an individual to ring that bell. To do so is to quit–there are no second chances, no do-overs. You ring the bell, take off your helmet, place it on the ground below the bell, turn, and leave.

Since my youth, there has been an evolution in training and warfare. However, one thing that has remained constant is the refusal to quit and the determination to overcome any obstacles. This story is more than an invaluable lesson of never giving up despite encountering seemingly insurmountable challenges. It's also about worse-case scenarios and impregnable walls. It too, is about our youth and their lack of instruction for transitioning from adolescence to adulthood. Finally, it is about the wall I currently face hindering me from reaching my goal. This magnificent goal is to create a program, a "Rite of Passage,"[1] offered to a specific group of individuals, similar to a "Hero's Journey." It's aim, to provide an experience akin to the one I had at BUD/S, guiding an entire generation who is transitioning from adolescence to adulthood.

The current challenge I face, is to secure funding for my program. This challenge has presented as an impregnable wall for which I must find another solution in order to move forward. I've been working on creating a real-world, nature-based, fully immersive "Rite of Passage"[2] program for youth 18, 19, and 20 that operates year-round as a live-in experience. The program is part of my own 501 (C) 3 non-profit organization called "Honor Bound Academy."[3] So this is a story, presenting an alternate solution that takes a different direction to bypass the wall in my way. In it, I'll describe this new solution using these very words to share the knowledge and insight I've gathered to aid you and your generation as you journey into adulthood. At the same time, I will continue my responsibility to seek the finances for a real-world Academy that you will eventually see, touch, feel, and believe in.

As you transition from adolescence to adulthood, you will encounter numerous impregnable walls in the form of daunting challenges. As mentioned before, at the age of nineteen, I had a unique experience that involved a bell. I was given the opportunity to be pushed to my limits in a controlled environment, surpassing what I thought I could achieve. This experience showed me that regardless of our skills, luck always plays a role. Some of you may not need what I have to offer, as you may be fortunate enough to successfully transition to adulthood without it. Unfortunately, many of you will not be lucky. You may strive to achieve your magnificent goals only to encounter numerous obstacles. That is why I sought to establish a supportive environment where you could be mentored, as I was, by experienced individuals at the start of your journey. An Academy staffed with mentors bound by honor would push you to your limits but not beyond, using wisdom and insightful knowledge. In the days of old when nine out of ten citizens were agrarian, there were naturally constructed "Rites of Passage"[4] that were created to guide youth in a controlled setting, such as a farm or ranch, as youth began their journey toward adulthood. Today's modern alternative for our youth's passage is something akin to a swift kick in the shorts and a condescending "Good Luck."

I will never give up, it's not my nature. In truth, I will not give up because of what I was offered, compassionate, unconditional guidance as a gift from a generation of youth. This brings me here, to return the gift and seek a direct connection with you. You, Americas youth, have awoken in me a desire to bring all my talents and tools to bear. In order to confront the current situation I'm facing concerning funding. From those I've sought support who have erected barriers, secure behind their mighty walls, confident in their wealth, preventing me from giving you "Honor Bound Academy."[5] These are the funders, wealthy donors, and patrons. Though they've clearly understood my presentation each time I've had the opportunity to present it, it appeared that they lacked proper motivation to lend their support. Regardless, these mighty titans cannot stop me from providing you with the necessary information drawn by sharing this story. Had it been the best-case scenario, this information would have been taught at physical locations scattered throughout the country. Under the name "Honor Bound Academy," [6] each attendee would have experienced a unique curriculum taught during a 365-day odyssey of self-determination, self-discovery, and self-awareness, ultimately leading to a spiritual awakening.

Chapter Two

SHIFTING PERSPECTIVE

To paint a picture in your mind, let's start by discussing the concepts through use of micro and macro. The micro represents the "Rite of Passage"[7] program called "Honor Bound Academy, Inc."[8] The macro considers the purpose of such an academy and the perspective it offers our youth preparing to enter the real world. Over the past thirty-five years, I've observed a change in our society. I see in today's youth the same potential and talent that our grandparents and parents possessed. However, there's a perception these youth are not ready for the responsibilities of adulthood. This perception is based on the perspectives of most adults and is rooted in their reality, not yours.

Why do some people, especially elders, believe that you are not ready for adulthood despite having the same talents, abilities, and intelligence as those who have come before you? I'd be curious to hear their thoughts on this question, as I have given it considerable thought myself.

In the following pages, I will attempt to connect the micro with the macro concepts while keeping it simple. I will begin by defining the word "precept," according to Merriam-Webster's Dictionary: "1. a command or principle intended especially as a general rule of action." A precept can also be understood as a principle governing action or procedure and a rule of behavior commonly accepted as a valid guide.[9]

With this understanding, I offer a single precept, defined from three different sources, to establish our starting point.

> First: "With all things being equal, the simplest explanation tends to be the right one. Occam's Razor—William of Ockham."[10] This is also called the law of parsimony.
>
> Second: "Once you eliminate the impossible, whatever remains, no matter how improbable, must be the truth."[11] Sir Arthur Conan Doyle, Sr.
>
> Third: "No. Try not. Do... or do not. There is no try."[12]
>
> —YODA, *Star Wars: Episode V–The Empire Strikes Back.*

These three perspectives establish a single, anchored starting point for a "Rite of Passage."[13] This journey will discard the distracting fiction of modern adolescence and reveal the simple fact that adolescents are fearless. By removing the impossible and improbable, a truth of whether to do or not will materialize, ultimately leading to the one essential ingredient: a "Strategic Vision." For those of you ready for adulthood and do not need guidance from these words, I offer you a suggestion before parting.

> "Follow your bliss. If you do follow your bliss, you put yourself on a kind of track that has been there all the while waiting for you, and the life you ought to be living is the one you will live. When you can see that, you begin to meet people who are in the field of your bliss, and they open the doors to you. I say, follow your bliss and don't be afraid, and doors will open where you didn't know they were going to be. If you follow your bliss, doors will open for you that wouldn't have opened for anyone else."
>
> —JOSEPH CAMPBELL[14]

For those of you who may not be ready, or perhaps are unsure, I offer a plan of attack in the following chapters. It will be based on the simplicity of examining the past through the lens of the stated precept (Strategic Vision), with the purpose of understanding today's world in order to foresee your future.

> "It is not the critic who counts; not the man who points out how the strong man stumbles, or where the doer of deeds could have done them better. The credit belongs to the man who is actually in the arena, whose face is marred by dust and sweat and blood; who strives valiantly; who errs, who comes short again and again, because there is no effort without error and shortcoming; but who does actually strive to do the deeds; who knows great enthusiasms, the great devotions; who spends himself in a worthy cause; who at the best knows in the end the triumph of high achievement, and who at the worst, if he fails, at least fails while daring greatly, so that his place shall never be with those cold and timid souls who neither know victory nor defeat.
>
> —THEODORE ROOSEVELT, Speech at the Sorbonne, Paris, April 23, 1910"[15]

As we continue, answer me this: what do all video games have in common? You are correct if you answered that they are all challenging, test your skills, rely on electrical currents, and are based on winning or losing. It does not matter whether the system is a PC, XBOX, PS, or Wii. I have another question to ask, if you will. What do life and the vast majority of these video games have in common? If you said challenging, electrically charged, centered on winning or losing, and overcoming adversity, then what follows is written just for you, especially if you are eighteen, nineteen, or twenty.

To all of you eighteen, nineteen, or twenty-year-olds: you are standing at the threshold of the greatest game you will ever play—adulthood. There will be no greater challenge that will test all your skills and is ultimately formatted as a duality to either win or lose. The difference between the games you play on a device and the game of life is simple: life is not easily reset.

What's the point of all of this you ask? For the better part of your young life, you've been instructed on how to become an adult. Your education, for the most part, has been the same thing over and over again. Let me ask you, does it sound something like this—you need to get good grades, stay out of trouble, don't have sex, finish high school, and especially don't use drugs?

Ok, you've heard all this before, and you understand it. That's good. Let me try this word on you—"spiritual." All the lessons you've been given so far throughout your lives come from the philosophical or technical perspective using 0's and 1's (Binary) to explain everything. They spoke to you as a matter of fact. In other words, it was presented in only two possible states, "off and on" or "black and white" regarding what can be known. Those same lessons may also be given spiritually, falling into a category often referred to as the grey area or what is unknown but cannot be discounted. That is why these words or lessons will be different. Unlike the wonderful world of video games, life is not black and white, so be warned that this world you're entering, is not what you think it is.

Are you still interested? Let's explore the difference between spiritual and philosophical. For those of you still following along, let's ensure we're on the same page and see if we can find mutual understanding. First, let's consider spirituality, understanding that it differs from religion. Let's look at it through the grey lens, allowing us to contemplate life from a different perspective.

With this different view, answer me this: "Why are we experiencing a society so lost and confused?" "How do we find ourselves adrift at the start of the 21st Century?" I don't want you to think that I'm saying it is easy to sum up the world's problems simply by shifting your perspective from the philosophical to the spiritual, but let's give it a shot. To comprehend today regarding these issues, we must look at yesterday. For the sake of expediency, let's choose a moment from the past. Let's consider the time in history known as the cultural revolution that was the Renaissance. A wonderous time of transition from the Middle Ages to modernity. But was it truly a wonderful time to be alive? During this period, something else was going on that did not make it into the history books. There was an evolution of sorts, whereby, at the end of the Renaissance, humanity was experiencing what is described as a loss of meaning due to the lack of cosmic vision (Big Picture). Implicitly, science was being viewed as if it could answer anything, and what was not being answered was seen as not existing at all. This attitude has resulted in us becoming deeply immersed in the material world, where presently we awaken each day.

Centuries ago, a lack of awareness led to a crisis that has escalated. Newton's law prevailed for a long time before Einstein's theory of relativity took over. This focus on the material world has resulted in a loss of personal identity, meaning, and connection. As young future leaders, you are paying the ultimate price by living in a material world gone insane. Right now, just as we all did in our youth when we believed in magic, there are moments when you feel an electrical pulse all around you, leaving you wanting more. You see amazing and meaningful things that do not make sense because you seek understanding through the abstract language of 1's and 0's in the technology you wield. For you to gain insight into the realm of magical and mystical, you will need to change our binary language of the material world, for the language of the unconscious or spiritual world.

Chapter Three

PATTERNS FROM THE PAST

Both philosophy and spirituality offer ways to explore the truth about human existence and experience. The main difference is that philosophy relies on a cognitive rationale approach, while spirituality is rooted in an affective emotional approach. In simple terms, philosophy is of the brain, and spirituality is of the soul. Long ago, we lost our connection, our meaning, and our identity to the scientific world of materialism.

How can we regain that understanding? Is there a language that is not abstract, a language that can help us comprehend the emotions, magic, and amazement associated with the electrical impulses that surround us? I have always been fascinated by Carl Gustav Jung and his theories about the unconscious, especially the collective unconscious and synchronicity. To illustrate, I'll share from personal experiences.

This next segment is about legacy. It may or may not make sense to those of you who are now at the threshold of your life's journey. Fear not, in time, it will be better understood. For now, I ask that you stay with me, soon I will bring it back to a place where you will have a clear understanding. By sharing my reflections, personal experiences, and past memories from the timeframes of my twenties, thirties, forties, fifties, and sixties, I hope to create a new understanding. I aim to identify patterns and gain insight from hindsight. The experiences I share will help explain the strong emotions evoked by the surrounding electrical pulses of life that make you feel and believe in magic.

My journey commenced with Basic Underwater Demolition/SEAL (BUD/S) training. I began at age nineteen and completed the training six months later at twenty. I found my way to BUD/S during Navy boot camp. In the third week, we were allowed to take a screening test. With me came an individual to share this adventure, he had been born and raised in the town of Coronado, CA. He had joined specifically to become a SEAL; I had no idea what a SEAL was. I joined the Navy to become a Hospital Corpsman. We both went on the day of the test; I passed, but he did not. Was that synchronicity, consciousness, unconsciousness, or just by chance?

During my time at BUD/S, my classmates and I came to understand the importance of nature, especially the nature of water. It is powerful, dangerous, serene, conscious, or you may see it as unconscious. Regardless, learning to operate in nature taught me valuable lessons. For instance, nature is capable of taking your life or protecting you and your life. It all depends on how you perceive it. Water is what makes Navy SEAL's unique, and I'm here to tell you another fact: water communicates, especially in the surf zone. If you have any doubts, just ask a surfer.

At the age of twenty-nine, I was discharged from SEAL Team One for drug use, which was a mighty failure and a devastating blow. I started my thirties in a recovery facility (Project Ninety[16]), where I spent ninety days breaking my addiction to Crystal Meth, marijuana, beer, booze, and a serious case of resentment. I learned that with addiction, you cannot win or make the necessary changes using physical tools, physical force, or knowledge from the material world. You overcome your use of substances and the behaviors they cause by letting go and shifting your focus from a philosophical to a spiritual perspective. You create a completely different set of tools that'll change behaviors and allow for the release of past burdens. The key to change, if you are an addict or alcoholic, comes in the act of making amends to those you've harmed. In doing this, your soul begins to awaken since it truly thrives on truth. The truth is, in the past, we often lied, cheated, and stole, creating crises in our lives and the lives of others, especially those we love the most. By acknowledging the truth, we also come to a profound understanding. When we are truthful with others, we find we can become truthful with ourselves. We find in our own truth that we are likable, trustworthy, and unique. We also begin to grasp that we deserve to be held in esteem, not only by others but most importantly by ourselves.

My initial attempt at transitioning from adolescence to adulthood was a path of learning, embracing, and pursuing mastery over nature's energy, only to have it all taken away due to drug use. In my thirties, I needed to re-think how I saw and was living life. It was necessary to begin a new journey, one of redemption. I had not only destroyed my military career but my identity. Being a SEAL was not just what I did, it was who I was, and now, never to be again. My thirties were spent changing my perspective. It was as radical of a change as can be imagined. My belief in powers and energies that could not be seen but that I knew to exist did not change. As a SEAL, I found it in nature, especially with water. In recovery, it became apparent when I sought a power greater than myself, again not in religion but in spirituality. What I came to comprehend as a personal belief is an understanding of having two wills, the first my will, the second being the will of a power greater than I. There is also an understanding that "we are as our surroundings dictate." To lie, cheat, or steal is to be surrounded with negative energy. To conduct yourself with kindness, sincerity, and love is to be surrounded with positive energy. I leave it to you to decide whether these suggestions I've offered are a choice, synchronicity, conscious, unconscious, or if it is all just by chance.

Two things occurred in this decade that began to form a new identity for me. My new journey was magnificent and mysterious. It is this way when you attempt to answer the big questions that life has for all of us, such as, "Who am I?" "What is my purpose?" and "How should I live?" The jobs I took post-military were chosen to support my sobriety. In the first four years I worked at an adolescent recovery facility, Daytop Village[17], along with four additional years at a Boys & Girls Club[18], I found my purpose from all the many youths and their gift of true friendship. In this way I would dedicate my life to adolescents because I believed my sobriety was due in large part to the trust they, or you, have in me. There was also a physical journey. After eight years, I wanted to write a book about my experiences, so I set out to crisscross America.

I started by walking northward along the Pacific Crest Trail (PCT).[19] I also hitch-hiked, took buses, and drove a bit. I did all this to acquire additional research on youth, gain new insights, and further understanding. The idea was to have it culminate with employment at the Boys & Girls Club of America, Corporate Offices located in Atlanta, Georgia.[20] As I saw it, the journey would end with a book of all my adventures in writing, along with my arrival on Peachtree Street, downtown Atlanta. As planned, two years later, with my completed book in hand, I made an appointment to see about a job. It had taken serious willpower to accomplish this task, a great deal of fortitude, dedication, and discipline. As was shared previously, when it comes to our will, there are two—my powerful will and the will of a power greater than myself. My attempt at securing a job with the corporate office was not successful. A bachelor's degree, which I did not possess, was required for employment. Rather than continued service to youth with a job in management at the corporate level, I was redirected toward academia. Again I wonder—was this synchronicity, the conscious, unconscious, or just by chance? Your thoughts?

At the age of thirty-eight, I began studies for a bachelor's degree, which I completed at the age of forty. During that same year I began my graduate studies in Social Work. At forty-two, I graduated with a Master of Social Work and began collecting hours for licensure. Then, at the age of forty-five, I had completed the required hours and passed the exam to be a Licensed Clinical Social Worker. Two years later, I attained Board Certification as a Diplomate in Clinical Social Work.[21] What started all those years ago as my transition from adolescence to adulthood in uncertainty, indecision, and bewilderment had evolved to having meaning and purpose. Again, can it be defined as Carl Jung's synchronicity, the conscious and unconscious, or is it just by chance?

In my fifties, I worked in various roles utilizing my credentials, including Child Protective Services (CPS), working with the disabled at Sonoma Developmental Center (SDC), Veterans Home of California Yountville with a geriatric community, California Department of

Corrections (CDC-R), and a DoD Contractor working as a Military and Family Life Consultant (MFLC).[22] During that decade, I honed all the necessary skills to be at my best for the youth I've dedicated my life to. As a clinical therapist I have pursued knowledge that enhances and establishes successful outcomes. I've learned through every experience. At this stage, I'd honed my therapeutic skills most effectively to address transitional issues, including post-traumatic stress disorder (PTSD), anxiety, addiction, and adolescence. I use as a primary modality cognitive behavioral therapy (CBT), but I find what works best for those I serve is eye movement desensitization reprocessing (EMDR), brain spotting, and hypnosis. All these models have proven to be very effective. I have followed what works best for me, regardless of where it leads me. It has been well planned out. The question is, was the plan mine or something else? Again — could it be Jung's synchronicity, the conscious, unconscious, or by chance? Curiosity wonders what others think about this? Whether your life has unfolded consciously, unconsciously or is your life one of random chance?

Having now entered my seventh decade of existence, I'm able to see life from a unique perspective. As I reflect on the past, I can now see patterns that have emerged that were not apparent to me when I was younger. There is a pattern of creating an identity, then dismantling it, only to rebuild it again, never yielding and never giving up. I have been fueled by two types of power: my own and the willpower of the one that is greater than I. It made no difference whether in the physical world or the spiritual realm, as they both showed patterns where all interactions appear to be governed, regardless of my awareness. This is my belief, derived from observations I've had through experiencing a lifetime of real-world circumstances. Pivotal situations, such as being discharged as a Navy SEAL for drug use, have had a significant impact on my life. Looking back, I realize that if I hadn't been discharged, I would not be who I am today. Like my BUD/S classmates, I would have remained in the military and retired in my mid-forties. This would have meant no opportunity for education, no professional licensure, and no formative youthful life experiences. Perhaps there would have been some meaning, but the sense of purpose I now possess would not exist.

As I share with you, I can see interventions at various times in my life. It appears that I was guided all along, from a chance meeting in boot camp to the discharge and the devastating loss of an early identity. In retrospect, was it I who took the bull by the horns, creating a path, vanquishing all foes, and achieving success from defeat, or was it Jung's synchronicity, the conscious and unconscious, or was it, you know, just by chance?

To the youth—those of you at the beginning of what will be your "Hero's Journey,"[23] I now return my focus. To the rest of you seeking a better understanding, I'll continue as the near future unfolds. I've chosen to focus on those aged eighteen, nineteen, and twenty for a specific reason. As the knowledge unfolds in the pages that follow, I will reveal why your age is so critical. Along those same lines, other questions that arise will be addressed from a spiritual orientation. There is also a reason for this; all the answers will become clear before long. For the time being, choice, respect, and truth are all that matter. You, our nation's youth, are coming of age in a time that has no prior comparison for shedding light on the choices you will be asked to make.

Chapter Four

NONE OF US ARE AS GOOD, AS ALL OF US

Moving along, let's start the process of finding successful paths to begin this heroic journey of yours. Because choice is an absolute, I offer you two groups of names. Each group represents a path you can take to become admired, respected, and so importantly, trusted adults. With one group you will easily recognize the names; with the other, I am not so sure.

The first group of names is path "A":

Beyonce Knowles	Tavi Gevinson	Taylor Lautner	Shane Smith
Jenji Kohan	Sophia Amoruso	Mark Zuckerberg	LeBron James
Michelle Phan	Sheryl Sandberg	Evan Spiegel	Taylor Swift
Jenna Marbles	Lady Gaga	Freddie Wong	Elon Musk

The first group of names is somewhat familiar; they exemplify musicians, movie stars, athletes, internet entrepreneurs, and business moguls, or in other words, titans of American popular culture. They have each risen to the pinnacle of their chosen professions. None of them was given the status they enjoy; they all earned it. They worked hard, persevered, and continually overcame all obstacles and challenges. They did not give up, give in, or stop trying. They are worthy of our admiration and emulation. This path is available to every one of you.

The second group of names is path "B"

William Kyle Carpenter	Salvatore A. Guinta	Robert J. Miller	Michael P. Murphy
Leroy A. Petry	William D. Swenson	Jason L. Dunham	Michael A. Monsoor
Ty M. Carter	Dakota Meyer	Jared C. Monti	Ryan M. Pitts
Clinton L. Romesha	Kyle J. White	Ross A. McGinnis	Paul R. Smith

This second group of names you may not be as familiar with. They represent a cross-section of Americans from East, West, South and North. They have each risen to prominence through actions taken while under duress. Each name you read is a recipient of the Congressional Medal of Honor.[24] None of them was given the status they hold; to each recipient, it was awarded. Like the first group, they worked hard, persevered, and continually overcame all obstacles, and in the case of seven of these individuals, they gave their lives. They did not give up, give in, or stop trying. They are worthy of our admiration and emulation. This path, too, is available to every one of you.

As you stand at the threshold of adulthood, these two paths are representative of the initial direction you'll eventually take. The difference between the two paths can be found in motivation. The first path is driven by the motivation of "me" or first-person narrative. It's derived from our early history, the one that focuses on the American Cowboy or Lone Ranger. The rugged individual who sets out to blaze new trails, overcoming all adversity and challenges, doing so for individual glory. The second path is driven by the motivation of "we," or a third-person narrative with individuals that also set out to blaze new trails, overcoming all adversity and challenges, yet are remiss of personal glory. It derives from the original architects, the founders, who declared in order to form a more perfect union, sacrifice would be necessary for "We the People."

The freedom of choice is a human birthright. Whether this statement is understood philosophically or spiritually, it is now yours to make. Regardless of this choice, knowledge is the fundamental requirement for all success. The knowledge suggested to you through these words will have a greater effect on the second path of "we" rather than the first path of "me." This is because it is spiritually based and utilizes a unique perspective found throughout the "Electric Universe."[25] Everything that is offered will aid you on your path. If something is unclear, additional information will be provided for further clarification. Additionally, should hardships become overwhelming, you can always seek understanding from your like-minded peers. What brings solace to the sacrifices of each path is my belief that "none of us is as good as all of us."

> "When one is seeking something that is impossible to find or about which nothing is known. In such moments, all well-meant, sensible advice is completely useless—advice that urges one to try to be responsible, to take a holiday, not to work so hard (or to work harder), to have more (or less human contact), or to take up a hobby. None of that helps, or at best rarely. There is only one thing that seems to work: and that is to turn directly toward the approaching darkness without prejudice and total naiveté, and try to find out what its secret aim is and what it wants from you."[26]

As this journey continues, I'll share that I am not asking you to trust me; instead, I am asking you to give me the opportunity to earn your trust. Once that is stated, I'll move forward in an attempt to create a solid foundation of knowledge and insight. I'll do this by establishing dual aspects to the singular issue of "what's really going on?" First is the actual truth concerning our nation; the second is not so much the truth but rather a deceptive truth spun for mass consumption. I awake each day to see these two things as they battle for supremacy. One is vital for survival—yours, mine, and ours. I see that first version of the truth, the one found through hard work, cross-referencing, and research, attained tenaciously by digging deep. I also see the second version of the same truth, the deceptive truth, the one being spoon-fed to me and every other American from pathological liars, purveyors of half-truths, exaggerators, and whisperers of bold-faced lies, along with the spinning by embellishers through lies of omission for the very heart and soul of this great nation. To maintain the purpose of the original gift, along with its unconditional nature, I've sought to re-acknowledge the two aspects of this competing truth, making clear why it requires a wordsmith, a raconteur of mysteries, a storyteller weaving a mystical, magical, mysterious story. What is at stake is not just any story but our story, America's story. When describing "what is really going on in our nation," it is essential to be truthful, honest, and speak from the heart. The information shared will be fact-checked and, as often as possible, shared from personal, authentic experience. Without trust, we are lost. With trust, we are formidable.

To this nation's youthful future leaders, regardless of stature, the Motto for all the various "Honor Bound Academy's"[27] is Vincit Qui Se Vincit (it translates to "He conquers who conquers himself").[28] Come along as the picture continues to develop and this story unfolds. Before me, I see a "Founding Father." I'm sitting in Lodge #14 in quiet contemplation amongst the Brotherhood of Free Masonry. I, as an entered apprentice am seated in the South, across the room, directly in front of me and to the North a portrait of the Continental General, 1st President of the United States, and Master Mason George Washington in full masonic regalia. It has always been clear there is a price to be paid for speaking truth to power. I can only imagine what it was like for the Founding Fathers, who were constantly under siege, with fear as a constant companion. For example, Benjamin Franklin spoke succinctly when he stated: "We must all hang together, or most assuredly we shall all hang separately."[29] Furthermore, it was not only speaking the truth but also engaging in war as a rag-tag scrum facing the British, a full-fledged superpower.

I believe each Mason has their own reason for seeking fellowship in the fraternity of Free Masonry. For me, it was to be part of something bigger than myself. I also appreciated that it wasn't a secret organization but an organization that kept secrets. It, too, was important that there were principles Masonry subscribed to, such as "Brotherly Love, Relief and Truth"[30] (commonly found in English language rituals) or

"Liberty, Equality, Fraternity."[31] Years before, I had been part of a different organization, one that was steeped in traditions going back to the founding of our country. This organization was the United States Navy, and within its structure were organizations or commands that were not secret but kept secrets. Organizations, such as Fleet Forces, Military Sea Lift, Naval Forces Central, and several others. With me, it was the Naval Special Operations Command (SOCOM). Having participated in Basic Underwater Demolition/SEAL (BUD/S) training and graduating from Class 106, I became a member of this Fraternity, the Fraternal Order of UDT/SEALs.

When the career ended there was no longer an active brotherhood, but one that only met a couple times a year. It also depends on location; you might go years without crossing paths with a teammate or classmate. The two organizations, UDT/SEAL and Free Masonry, shared many aspects with one another, especially brotherhood. For me, I wanted to replace my naval codes of 8492[32] / 5326[33] for another code, initially as an Entered Apprentice Mason (1st Degree),[34] presently transitioned to Fellowcraft Mason (2nd Degree), and in due time becoming a Master Mason (3rd Degree).[35]

Chapter Five

WHAT'S REALLY GOING ON?

N ow, we come to the place where that question will not only be asked but answered. The question first mentioned in the Prologue requiring clarification and illumination. It's the one that we either can't see or refuse to see. Look now, America, at the six o'clock national news. Choose CNN, MSNBC, or Fox; it does not matter. Ask yourself if you are seeing the honest and absolute truth. If you say yes, then you can stop reading and drop this soliloquy in the trash bin. If, indeed, you're not sure that what you're seeing is the actual truth, then keep on reading. If you are still with me, then it's time to delve into the question. That question is simply this: "What's really going on?" Here, in the United States of America.

Continuing to build on the foundation that I've begun to establish; we'll now attempt to understand the question so necessary and vital. I'll do it as suggested earlier, allowing for the greatest probability of success, its form, a soliloquy. There's been a discussion regarding "The Founding Fathers, the Fraternal Order of Free Masons, and UDT/SEALs. Along with that is the request for an opportunity to earn your trust. I'm going to continue our conversation with additional knowledge in an attempt to understand the statement, "What's really going on?" The question applies to what's going on with this nation and its people, including, most importantly, those in transition from adolescence to adulthood.

I wish to point out the combination of three distinct words regarding myself, my past, and the youth I serve. I've shared working at Daytop Village, a recovery facility for youth. Following that, I worked as a Unit Director of the Boys & Girls Club of America. After these two experiences I returned to school and earned both a bachelor's and a master's degree. From there, I became a Licensed Clinical Social Worker (LCSW). Afterward, I accomplished board certification as a Diplomat in Clinical Social Work (BCD). Hence, from the experiences of my military career, education, and credentials comes the combination of three distinct words defining the role I play as: an "Adolescent Combat Diplomate."

Our nation is currently being governed by individuals who seek to divide us rather than unite us, acting more like Charlatan's or Exploiter's rather than leaders. I trust my instincts and feel that I should stick to what I know best. I want to focus further on the past decades I've lived through and share other personal experiences, particularly those involving youth and the adolescent condition.

It is important to recognize that the decision to focus on addressing our youth comes from personal and professional observations. We often tend to overlook our youth despite their presence before our very eyes. If we're truly going to be successful, it is essential to first step into their shoes and empathize with them. If we're afraid, then imagine how they must feel. I share this based on my extensive personal experience and the knowledge that there is fear at the core of every human being. Whether young or old, we are all creatures driven by fear. Few emotions affect our well-being as profoundly as fear does. It all boils down to one of two powerful characteristics at the heart of fear. One, is when we believe that something we possess is going to be taken from us. Or, second, we believe that something is going to be denied to us—something we truly believe should be ours, but is kept from us. This is where it begins and ends for all human beings. What do you think it is like to stand in the shoes of our youth, all whose lives we say matter to us and whom we acknowledge as our national treasures?

Let's start by asking what has and continues to be taken from them. For example, their schools, during and long after the COVID-19 Pandemic. These pillars of knowledge have been severely disrupted despite their crucial roles in modern society. These include socialization, social integration, social placement, and social/cultural innovation. The list is long and heartbreaking, so let's just take a glance as we move on. For kindergarteners, on their first day of school, there was no in-person teacher and no in-person friends–only virtual socialization. Then there are the elementary, middle, and high school graduations, experienced at home with family but no friends. Students are and have been separated from their friends, also disrupted are the after- school functions like glee club, science club, and sports. There were no proms, plays, or Friday night activities. There were no stadium lights, no crowds, and no friends in sight. Let's wrap this up with an apprehensive consideration of what is and has been denied our youth. Is it as straightforward as their childhood? Can we seriously doubt, as all assessments consistently point to a generation filled with anxiety and hopelessness.

Chapter Six

ADOLESCENT COMBAT DIPLOMATE

If I were to identify the pre-eminent threat to me, my loved ones, and society as a whole, it would be the division in this country. Right now, I see a nation confronted with deeds from our past that require serious attention. These include income inequality, racism, Black Lives Matter (BLM),[36] Me-Too Movements,[37] and the war on drugs, among other issues that are also of principal importance. I also see the masses turning on one another, feeling confused and dangerously disconnected. Most troublesome is what I'm not seeing, as I believe it is essential in altering these fearful feelings—it's leaders and leadership. I believe there are those among us, both men and women, who have yet to step up to address and confront these issues. It's as if they lay in troubled slumber. I've always taken pride in my ability to address the wreckage of my past due to mistakes I've made. Personally, I'm now fearful and anxious because I am not just facing my wreckage but the wreckage of this nation's past. I am sharing these words because I am tired of living in fear. If our nation needs strong leadership, I believe life should be an adventure, albeit a mysterious one, so count me in. Here and now let a banner of hope unfurl.

Joseph Campbell embraced three magical words regarding how to live a meaningful life, "Follow Your Bliss ."[38] Doing so has made my life a mysterious, adventurous, and meaningful journey. Over the last thirty-some odd sober years, as I reflect on the decades over which I've pursued my dream, I realize that I have filled those years with specific, meaningful, and interlocking accomplishments.

Critical for success is setting a cornerstone upon which a foundation can support not only the truth but the knowledge of the facts revealed. We do this from the beginning, reiterating the four years working in an adolescent recovery facility, observing, listening, and asking questions. The youth I interacted with during this time, ages thirteen to seventeen, gave my life meaning and purpose. Their unconditional gift of friendship teaching me how to "live, laugh, and love"[39] again. Most importantly, their friendship awakening me to believe in myself, to trust myself, and to forgive myself. Leaving the facility at Daytop Village, the precious embrace of their gifts continued with an opportunity to learn more from another group of youth—this time, their ages ranged from six to eighteen. I met these youths when I took a job as a Unit Director at the Boys & Girls Club of America, Paradise Valley, South San Francisco, California. Here, the responsibility was greater, as were the challenges. On my first day, the club membership consisted of fifty-nine young people. I worked there for an additional four years, and on my final day, our club membership was 440 kids. More than half were teenagers, and all of them were my responsibility. I had been trained in unconventional warfare as a Navy SEAL. I drew upon every bit of that Navy SEAL education to maintain my sanity, as I was given an education that I deemed infinitely more important than any other. Don't get me wrong, the defense of our nation is critical, but the well-being of our youth is substantially more vital. At the end of those eight years, the mysteries of life were fully embraced. I had learned how to live life without drugs or alcohol. I also found my calling, which led me on an adventurous journey of personal and professional discovery.

Ten years into my sobriety, at the age of thirty-eight, I shared my pursuit of higher education. At the age of forty, I graduated from Cornerstone University in Grand Rapids, Michigan, with a bachelor's degree in business administration. That same year, I entered the University of California Los Angeles (UCLA), School of Social Welfare. After graduation, armed with a Master's in Social Work (MSW) I was ready to change the world. My first professional job was with Child Protective Services (CPS) in Mariposa, California. My next job was at Sonoma Developmental Center (SDC), working with the developmentally disabled, and attaining credential. Once I gained licensure, I was able to secure jobs at the Veterans Home of California—Yountville and then the California Department of Corrections and Rehabilitation (CDC-R).

In 2009, I secured my dream job as a Military and Family Life Consultant (MFLC). In 2004, the United States military faced significant challenges with its personnel, families, and suicidal ideation due to war. Their solution was to hire clinical therapists to work alongside all branches of the military (Army, Navy, Marine, Corps, Air Force, and National Guard) stationed in the United States (CONUS) and abroad (OCONUS). In 2011, Special Operations Command (SOCOM) finally allowed the MFLC program to interface with Special Forces Operators and their families.

During my military service, I was a hospital corpsman and a Navy SEAL (8492[40]/5326[41]). If you recall, my discharge came in 1988, a time when the military saw drug use as a significant character defect. At that time, because the stigma was so powerful, anything having to do with mental health was avoided at all costs.

Isn't life strange? Or does it not work in mysterious ways? Regardless, doing the job of MFLC felt like being home, I took to this job as if I were born to it, which I was. I'd worked with the SEALs, the Green Berets, Rangers, Night-Stalkers, Raiders, and ParaRescue (PJ'S).[42] I'd spent a total of seven transformative years giving back and helping to change the culture. A culture that not long ago, saw mental health conditions as a weakness and as a stigma. Hooyah!

Moving forward from 2018, the world finds itself in the grip of the COVID-19 Pandemic. At this time, I worked at Sonoma Valley Community Health Center (FQHC), as an Integrated Behavioral Health Specialist (IBHS). My main responsibilities included supporting Homeless Outreach and evaluating patients experiencing Anxiety (GAD-7),

Depression (PHQ-9, as well as those with Drug (DAST) and Alcohol (AUDIT) dependencies. I have consistently striven to expand my knowledge, obtain further certifications, and give back with no thought of remuneration. I've volunteered as a therapist, working with First Responders at the West Coast Post-Trauma Retreat (WCPR) twice a month. I am now a Board-Certified Diplomate in Clinical Social Work, which includes a certification for War Trauma (CWT) through the American Academy of Experts in Traumatic Stress (AAETS). I also have a certification from the Eye Movement Desensitization Reprocessing International Association (EMDRIA). EMDR is the primary model utilized at the retreat. At WCPR, they are addressing First Responders experiencing severe Post Traumatic Stress Incidents (PTSI). With all of this linked end to end showing just how specific, meaningful, and interlocking accomplishments can serve its purpose.

Chapter Seven

WHY A MYSTERY?

To bind us all, one to another, as we begin our mutual odyssey, I offer the words of another visionary regarding this fundamental question: Why do humans need mystery as part of life? "It's intrinsic for us to seek answers. It's our evolutionary heritage, moving us forward by motivating us to find out more and use our imagination." Mystery is the ultimate trail of breadcrumbs, inviting us to solve or make sense of something and use our imagination to fill in the gaps. "'The need for mystery,' wrote American author Ken Kesey, 'is greater than the need for an answer.' In a time where there is great emphasis on proof, answers, and outcomes, the mystery persists as a reminder to enjoy the process—that undirected, unsettling, unknowable journey. Certainly, in our controlled culture we will be dissuaded from walking in the dark lest we bump, break, or be sued by somebody. Do it anyway. When the lights get too bright, we are programmed to seek the shadows, to nurture the unknowable, and, as Kesey states, 'to plant gardens in which strange plants grow and in which mysteries bloom.' (https://www.psychologies. co.uk/self/why-mystery-matters.html)" [43]

For those of us preparing for battle, "a sense of mystery is like no other feeling. It seems to light up the brain in a unique way. It is hard to describe the emotion, but it is clear that people enjoy the feeling. Why else would movies, television, and literature thrive when presenting a good mystery? We humans like to figure things out, and when there is no apparent answer, we like to look deeper to find out what is truly happening. In a way, the sense of mystery may be one of the most intriguing emotions of all."[44] We'll continue with the mystery, but to stay on task I'm going to introduce the necessary mechanisms of finance, physics, and their effect on our material world.

To you our youth, whether we like it or not, we must follow the money. I will be brief in making this point, but power and profit are key factors in understanding how we arrived at the present-day United States. More importantly, if we want to find solutions to our modern-day problems, focusing on power and profit presents a captivating opportunity. "Do you really want to do this? Do you want to put yourself out on a limb? Do you have the audacity to think you're smart enough, despite the abundance of naysayers pointing fingers in their rage, yelling, and screaming," how dare you think anyone wants to hear what you have to say?" Yes, it's a free country, and haven't we been told since a very young age that we live in America, where, if you're willing to work hard, be disciplined, and maintain focus, then anything is possible? Okay, if we're going to do this right, let's do it by jumping into the deep end. Let's start with power, profit, and the Military Industrial Complex (MIC).[45]

With focus and determination the journey continues, specifically for those who'll make up the vanguard—those that are the chosen ages of eighteen, nineteen, and twenty. For those of you too, of all other ages, who've felt that tingling sensation of curiosity, please let's continue onward. My experience with the military-industrial complex is through two specific interactions occurring decades apart. The first occurred with my enlistment in the United States Navy. I joined the service in 1979 during the Carter Administration, and within a year, it changed to the Reagan Administration. During this time, my pay increased from $78 dollars a week under Carter to $179 dollars a week under Reagan. Thank you, military-industrial complex. I benefitted further during this time frame due to Operation Eagle Claw, which eventually led to the creation of Special Operations Command (SOCOM). In 1980, I graduated from Basic Underwater Demolition/SEAL training (BUD/S Class

106) and was first stationed at NAB Little Creek and Underwater Demolition Team 22 (UDT-22). I observed a war-weary military that had ended the Vietnam War several years earlier. Morale was incredibly low but there was a need for the military to lift itself up by its bootstraps. It was the height of the Cold War and the military-industrial complex had to re-tool itself, which it did. During my first enlistment, I witnessed a broken, out of date military transition into a highly functional, unconventional Special Warfare tool.

In 2008, I had a unique job opportunity as a Military and Family Life Consultant (MFLC), marking my second interaction with the military-industrial complex. At this time, the military was grappling with war weariness and serious morale issues, particularly Suicidal Ideation (SI). The military-industrial complex has evolved significantly since 1980, largely due to the attacks of September 11, 2001. After leaving the military, I went back to school and became a Licensed Clinical Social Worker (LCSW). Because of my past experience as a Navy SEAL, I was sent to work with each of the branches Special Forces. I was inserted in the Command structure of the "Sky-Soldiers," "Green Berets," "Rangers (Scroll)," "Night-Stalkers," "Raiders," "PJ's," "Combat-Controllers (CCT), and Special Reconnaissance (SR)." [46] It was fascinating to observe the inner workings of these units, as they appeared almost corporate in their presentation. This was a remarkable transformation from my time as an Operator.

What really strikes me about this second interaction with the military-industrial complex is how the military has been privatized. There are now private corporations providing civilians for various military roles. Corporations such as Booz Allen, Halliburton, Blackwater (Academi), Leidos, and Magellan,[47] to name a few. For the moment, let's backtrack. Do you remember the statement "Power and Profit," along with the naysayers pointing fingers of rage? Rock the boat? Nobody likes it when we ask really hard questions, especially when the answers turn out to be different than previously believed, and that there is indeed another way, and this new way is actually better. It has to do with change and those who hold the reins of power. Those in power prefer the mass of humanity to remain dependent rather than become independent. Do you really think nothing will happen if we start digging around to find out where the actual power and profit reside, especially when considering the two distinct paths in which power and profit traverse? For our purposes, they are the legal and illegal aspects, both of which will dispatch all who should be so foolish as to impede upon either recipient's domain. So you see, the military industrial complex along with the numerous cartels of the world possess extraordinary wealth. Whether it's good or bad, right or wrong, each will respond to maintaining their power and profit in the same way, ruthlessly.

Chapter Eight

WE ARE HERE TO SERVE YOU

I have a deep understanding of the modern adolescent condition, and the difference from my own personal experiences as a youth. During my childhood society viewed children as they should be seen but not heard. Those memories are still so clear to me. I remember when changing the television channel required manual labor, when color television was brand new, and remote control was years away. Back then, my pops would tell us to change the channel, and whichever son was closest would stand and do as he was commanded, only asking, "what channel?" Ah-yes, during my childhood, the traditional family structure involved mothers staying at home while fathers provided for the family. During this time, not that long ago, a family could not only survive but thrive on a single income.

Being middle class and living in suburbia, I grew up sheltered and protected. Every year it was our family's custom to load up and drive 90 miles north for our annual two-week summer vacation at Russian River. During this time, we were surrounded by the entire extended family on my mom's side, who were all immigrants. This included grandparents, aunts, uncles, and numerous cousins.

These memories are powerful and innocent. Back then, everything felt safe and secure. At the end of summer, everyone returned home and started the new school year. During those times, most of us received our education in the public school system, which was considered pre-eminent throughout the world. Although I have fond memories of being protected from many of society's problems, those issues still existed and were looming on the periphery. However, I was not aware of them during my early childhood. It wasn't until the closing years of high school that alcohol consumption, drug use, and marital dysfunction became a personal reality, moving from the periphery to the forefront of our family, up close and personal.

The 1960s was a time of significant change in society. It was marked by both great achievements, such as the moon landing, and tragic events like the assassinations of President John F. Kennedy, his brother, Robert Kennedy, as well as civil rights leaders Medgar Evers, Malcolm X, and Dr. Martin Luther King, Jr. These events caused a noticeable strain on the innocence of the time, as society began to fray. This decade closed out, and a new one began, it was now the 1970's.

This new decade would see a different President resign in disgrace; an unpopular war (Vietnam) come to an end, nationwide implementation of public school busing, and severe gas shortages. Society continued undergoing significant change, but before that transformation fully took hold, there was a glimmer of hope, as the mighty Led Zeppelin made its grand appearance. Through the transition from adolescence to adulthood, my generation were guided by the magical, mystical, and mysterious lyrics filled with ancient energy, like: "In the days of my youth, I was told what it means to be a man. Now I've reached that age, I've tried to do all those things the best I can."[48] Even with all the insanity of the sixties and seventies, there was still optimism; families were struggling, but the illusion of wholeness persisted. Gas was .59 cents a gallon, housing was affordable, college was attainable, and dreams seemed to be within reach, but not for much longer. No mas! No mas!

This is how it began for me. My first two decades are very different from the prior two decades if you are 18, 19, or 20. To make the necessary change for our youths during the next two decades will require a call to arms, a summons to actively engage, an invitation or appeal to take a particular course of action. For our purposes, let us consider a social call to arms, in accord with each living American generation. In preparation, I now present an analysis of our citizens from the perspective of both asset and liability. To gain insight, we will explore the collective strengths and weaknesses of each generation, for better and worse. Sun Tzu,[49] describes a key element in the Art of War[50] as 'if you know the enemy and know yourself, you need not fear the results of a hundred battles."[51] Let's not deceive ourselves; today we are currently engaged in a daily war as we step out the front doors of our homes. Understanding each living generation is essential for favorable outcomes that we can depend on. The assets and liabilities need to be evaluated and assessed for their role in the upcoming battles. We are the grandparents, parents, brothers, sisters, aunts, and uncles of our youth.

For all youth, get to know us for the many ways we can serve you, beginning with the Greatest Generation—the elders of this movement. It's important to take a step back to see the big picture as we navigate our way towards effective change. Our living generations are as follows:

TIME FRAME	TITLE	DESCRIPTION
1901 to 1927	"The Greatest Generation"	Also known in American usage as the "G.I. Generation."[52]
1928 to 1946	"The Silent Generation"	Also known as the "Lucky Few" or "Traditionalist Generation."[53]
1946 to 1964	"Baby Boomers," "Boomer"	Also known as the ME Generation.[54]
1965 to 1980	"Generation X," "13ers"	Also known as "13th Generation" or "Gen X."[55]
1981 to 1996	"Millennials"	Also known as "Generation Y" (often shortened to Gen Y).[56]
1997 to Abt. 2012	"Generation Z"	Also known as "Gen Z" for short and colloquially as "Zoomers."[57]
Early 2010's to mid to late 2020's	"Generation Alpha"	Often shortened to "Gen Alpha."[58]

Chapter Nine

S.W.O.T.

We all have had or have grandparents, for me my grandparents belonged to the Greatest Generation, which is now dwindling as the last remaining members are reaching the century mark. They share admirable qualities such as personal responsibility, integrity, humility, strong work ethic, financial prudence, and faithful commitment. This generation wanted "to curb the power of capital, create economic growth and development, end poverty, and enable people to advance themselves."[52] If this generation had a weakness, it was leaving many of these wants or desires, unfinished. The greatest opportunity they have to offer is the manner in which they've lived their lives. "Most of these participants of the Great Depression,"[53] and World War II "fared unusually well in their adult lives. They came out of hardships of the Great Depression with an ability to know how to survive and make do by solving problems,"[54] a talent they still possess."

The threat is allowing them to go quietly into the night. They are an untapped asset that still has much to offer. If nothing else, they have stories still to share. By not taking advantage of what they represent, long-lived honorable American citizens, this is the greatest threat to all the generations who follow in their footsteps.

The Silent Generation is the generation of my parents, their war, Korea, and the start of the Cold War (Communist Russia—USSR). Unlike the previous generation who had fought for "changing the system,"[55] my parents' generation was about "working within the system. They did this by keeping their heads down and working hard; this is what earned them the "silent" label. Their attitudes leaned toward not being risk-takers and playing it safe."[56]

"From their childhood experiences during the Depression and the example of frugality set by their parents, Silents tended to be thrifty and even miserly,"[57] but in a good way. Their weakness, "whereas divorce in the eyes of the previous generation was considered aberrant behavior, the Silents were the generation that reformed marriage laws to allow for divorce and lessen the stigma. This led to a historically unprecedented wave of divorces among Silent Generation couples in the United States."[58]

"As a birth cohort, Silents never rose in protest as a unified political entity."[59] Because "following the rules" had proven to be successful for my parents generation, which led to incredible and stable wealth creation. It was inevitable that their Boomer and Gen X children would become estranged from them due to their different views."[60] Our rebellious nature, vocal social concerns, and economic hardship created a different generational consciousness, or as it is commonly referred to, "the generation gap."[61]

The opportunities that my parent's Silent Generation presents are numerous. They vote consistently, they have an abundance of time to share, and they are financially better off than many of the generations that succeeded them. There's also their sense of honor for distinguishing right from wrong, their moral compass nearly always finding true north. Of all the opportunities that are found with the Silent Generation, their pride in their country is unquestionable. They've lived through the Depression, and the civil rights era—remembering keenly what it was like prior to this movement when "Jim Crow" was the law of this land.

The threat is complicated, starting with the style of parenting they adopted with me and my siblings. Representative of this was the notion that "children should be seen but not heard." Boomers have gone on to raise our own children with various parenting styles. These conflicting views, often seen between us, caused many breaches within the family structure. Not the least of which was the effect of their normalizing divorce, leaving many old wounds still festering.

Next, we "Boomers grew up at a time of dramatic social change,"[62] our war Vietnam. We are also a huge generation, some 79 million strong. We account for a quarter of the total U. S. population. By sheer force of numbers, we almost certainly will redefine old age in America, just as we've made our mark on teen culture, young adult life, and middle age. We "boomers are characterized as being workaholics who relish long weekends and overtime."[63] It can be said that we're more committed to our roles than any other generation. We have a work ethic of 'work hard, play hard' and consider ourselves good team players.

Our weaknesses begin with a "preference for structure and discipline,"[64] and we aren't very good with change. We are also competitive, needing recognition to keep us motivated to achieve more. "At the moment, the Baby Boomers are pretty glum."[65] A full 80% say we're dissatisfied with the way things are going with the country today. "Boomers are also more downbeat than other adults about the long-term trajectory of our lives "[66] and our children's lives. We also suspect we played a pivotal role in the financial mess all the generations are presently experiencing.

The opportunities that Boomers present are endless. We have been shaped by the Vietnam War, along with the tensions from nuclear annihilation during the Cold War, the dawn of space exploration, and racial issues. We Boomers participated in the greatest social changes in the history of our country during the 1960s and 1970s. We brought about dramatic shifts in educational, social, and economic opportunities. By far, the greatest opportunity we present, one that is unbelievably crucial, is a voting block that can truly affect deep, meaningful change.

On the flip side, the threat we pose is in our numbers. "On January 1, 2011, the oldest Baby Boomers turned sixty-five. Every day from that date for the next nineteen years, about 10,000 more will cross that threshold. By 2030, when all Baby Boomers will have turned sixty-five, fully eighteen percent of the nation's population will be at least that age."[67] The increasing number of boomers will strain social services, "meaning one in five Americans will be considered a senior citizen."[68] We should consider that if indeed we've taken so much from society, it's only fair that we give back as much.

Now, in the United States Generation Xers or 13ers as in 13th generation, literally the 13th generation to call itself American, "are described as the major heroes of September 11 terrorist attacks. The firefighters and police responding to the attacks were predominately from Generation X."[69] The numbers of this generation "responded to the terrorist attacks with bursts of patriotism and national fervor that surprised even themselves."[70] This generation is committed to juggling work and family time and favors work-life balance as a staple of their lives.

In regard to weaknesses, Gen "Xers were children at a time when society was less focused on children and more focused on adults. Xers were children during a time of increasing divorce rates."[71] They "watched the decay and demise of the family and grew callous to the loss."[72] "This resulted in an increase in latchkey children,[73] as they were the "first to grow up without a large adult presence being more peer-oriented than previous generations."[74]

The opportunity that Generation X presents came from a study reporting that "by any measure, the least racist of today's generations."[75] In the workplace, they had to rise to the challenge, being asked "to adapt to the Boomers first, then to adapt to the millennials and Gen Z."[76] Having been caught between generations of greater numbers, their ability to adapt is an asset. "They are natural translators and remixers."[77] Research acknowledges Gen X "as highly effective in empathy, a critical success factor in today's multigenerational workplace."[78]

The threat is found in a different survey showing Gen Xers exhibit higher levels of cynicism and disaffection than previous generations. However, this can be said for the better part of our society at this time in our nation's history.

As we move on of all generations currently in the workforce, Millennials are considered the most independent. They are concerned with ethics and the social responsibility of the organization they work for.

This generation has grown up sourcing information; they need to be left to create their own processes rather than being told what to do.

Regarding their independent nature, Millennials are not as interested in teamwork as other generations. This generation is also impatient when it comes to career growth, being more likely to leave before two years if they feel their skills are not being developed. Millennials benefited the least from the economic recovery following the Great Recession. The nation's younger workers report earning 20% less than the generation before them; "not only did they receive lower wages, they also had to work longer hours for fewer benefits."[79] Furthermore, "the decline and disappearance of stable full-time jobs with health insurance and pensions for people who lack a college degree have had profound effects on working-class Americans, who now are less likely to marry and have children within marriage than those with college degrees."[80]

The opportunity amongst Millennials can be astonishing when it comes to their voting. Among millennials and the Obama era, "not only did they provide their votes but also the enthusiasm . . . volunteered in political campaigns, and donated money."[81]

The threat is twofold with the Millennial Generation. Despite the hype surrounding the political engagement and possible record turnout amongst young voters, millennials' voting power has had a glitch when considering "the comparatively higher number of them who are non-citizens."[82] Secondly, "while millennials are well known for taking out large amounts of student loans, these are actually *not* their main source of non-mortgage personal debt, but rather credit card debt."[83]

Then we have Generation Z, "the most technology competent of any generation; members of Gen Z are able to pick up new developments quicker than other employees."[84] This generation is particularly ambitious, with two-thirds of Gen Z saying their goal in life is to make it to the top of their profession.[85] Gen Z are natural entrepreneurs described as the "always on" generation.[86] Gen Z is able to multi-task, unlike any other generation, utilizing up to five screens at once."[87] This generation is generally more risk-averse in certain activities than earlier generations. As youth, fewer have tried alcohol and had lower teen pregnancy rates, less substance use, and higher on-time high school graduation rates.

When it comes to weaknesses, "Gen Z is regarded as more cynical than their predecessors, favoring a realistic outlook over the idealism of Generation Y."[88] "Unlike the millennials—who came of age during the Great Recession—this generation was in line to inherit a strong economy with record-low unemployment. That has all changed now, as COVID-19 has reshaped the country's social, political, and economic landscape. Instead of looking ahead to a world of opportunities, Gen Z now peers into an uncertain future. There are a litany of signs that the oldest Gen Zers have been particularly hard hit in the early and long-term effects of the coronavirus crises."[89]

The opportunity comes from hardship—the March of Our Lives was in 2018. This was Gen Z demonstrating their demand for stricter gun-control legislation following the Stoneman Douglass High School shooting. An opinion piece titled "Dear National Rifle Association: We Won't Let You Win, From, Teenagers,"[90] published in March 2018 in The New York Times, describes Generation Z as the generation after Millennials, who will "not forget the elected Officials who turned their backs on their duty to protect children of their generation."[91]

The biggest threat for this generation is global—it's climate change. Others would say "that the growing amount of time teens are spending on their mobile devices, and specifically on social media, is contributing to the growth in anxiety and depression among this group."[92] For those who see the effect of social media as truly harmful, "the most common reason cited is that it leads to bullying and rumor spreading."[93] Not only do those issues exist for Generation Z, but they are also unfamiliar with a time before social media and easily accessible technology, which can make them overly reliant on technology to solve problems.

I've looked at each living generation in present-day America. I've assessed each generation's strengths, weaknesses, opportunities, and threats, individually and collectively. As an "Adolescent Combat Diplomate," I am inspired to bring all that I am, all that I know, and all that I have become through the gifts of a generation that I've dedicated my life to serving. We are all part of an unparalleled social experiment called the "United States of America." This American experiment is unique and improbable, as our Founding Fathers, specifically Thomas Jefferson, penned the Declaration of Independence in 1776. We were thirteen colonies that defied Britain, the most powerful nation on earth at that time. Just look around the world at how difficult it is for democracy and freedom to take hold and flourish. We as Americans are a political miracle. I refuse to believe we are a nation in the process of collapse.

Chapter Ten

IT BEING AN AUTHENTIC TRUTH

As we maintain focus on the question of "what's really going on?" I previously stated in this soliloquy that "I want to be utterly, absolutely, and as brutally honest in what I reveal." Through careful consideration, I believe it is of utmost importance to first understand what an honest and genuine truth looks like. Second, by clarifying the two aspects as in truth, verse non-truth. As our example, I've chosen to apply three different circumstances that occurred not so long ago. This is where the veil was pulled back, allowing a clear view of the absolute truth regarding several powerful entities. These three situations allow us to see exactly what was going on, along with the price paid for speaking truth to power:

- The first, Julian Assange, editor, publisher and activist who founded WikiLeaks;[94]
- The second Edward Snowden;[95] and
- The third exposure of an absolute truth, the Panama Papers.[96]

*"Continuing with a mighty pen, using the written word
as an example for my generation of youthful Confidants.
History will either write you, or you will write history?"*

—TJLJR

The use of these documents will aid us in understanding what is clearly the truth. With this information having been released, starting in December of 2006, it gives us a chance to study authentic truth. The individuals named have paid an incredibly high price, for their selfless act. First was a website with the motto: "to publish fact-based stories without fear or favor. Yes, this is Wiki-leaks along with its editor Julian Assange, having released substantial documents pertaining to the US "War on Terror." The next disclosure of documents is from the man who spilled the NSA's secrets. A former systems administrator for the CIA, Edward Snowden, a private intelligence contractor, has also paid a severe price. The truth he revealed concerned the bulk collection of phone and internet data from US users. Along with this data, there are also personal communications and information gained from foreign governments, including those of our allies.

Let's step back and evaluate the information just presented. History has recorded the price that Julian Assange and Edward Snowden have paid. In speaking truth to power, they found themselves out on a limb, with no protection and nowhere to hide other than a prison cell. The final set of documents takes us on a journey into a strange and mysterious world of high finance, filled with a maze of smoke and mirrors. The third truth are the Panama Papers. They exposed the personal financial information of the wealthiest one percent of individuals, they also revealed the involvement of current and former world leaders, public officials, hundreds of celebrities, politicians, business moguls, and other wealthy individuals. The key to understanding the 'who,' 'what,' 'where,' 'when,' and 'why,' lies with the three individual whistleblowers. They have revealed the 'what,' which is the authentic truth. The 'where' was worldwide and in Germany the information was given to an investigative journalist, the 'who' was with the International Consortium of Investigative Journalists (ICIS).[97] The 'when' was the year 2014, and then the 'why'? Of all the disclosures, why were the Panama Papers so valuable? We shall follow the money to see that truth.

Let's look back at the year 2008, which is best described as the year when banks in America were too big to fail. Going back to this timeframe will give us a starting point in understanding what occurred in 2014 with the Panama Papers. The solution back then to this problem was a bailout for banks using taxpayer money. What I remember most about this debacle is what happened after the taxpayer funds were allocated and stability was attained. By Christmas of that same year, the purchasing of assets and equity had begun to stabilize the market. Having survived the financial crisis, those same banks and bankers who were considered "too big to fail" proceeded to award themselves a yearly bonus, using money from the Department of Treasury—essentially using the taxpayer's–money.

The sheer magnitude of money involved in understanding the power and profit of both legal and illegal monies found throughout the world, is daunting. For this reason, I'll focus on the three disclosures that leave no doubt of authenticity. By doing this I'll share what I believe creates such anxiety and feelings of hopelessness and helplessness in our youth.

Julian Assange, Edward Snowden, and John Doe of the Panama Papers are individuals, as well as whistleblowers. We know for sure that two paid a severe price, while the third is a question mark for bringing the truth into the light. Not just any truth, but the utterly, absolutely, and brutally honest truth. I found a saying that came to me while researching this information. These are those words:

> "The horrific magnitude of detriment to the world should shake us all awake. But when a whistleblower sounds the alarm, it is cause for even greater concern. It signals that democracy's checks and balances have all failed, that the break-down is systemic, and that severe instability could be just around the corner. So, now is the time for real action . . ."[98]

How do we bring to light that which causes such fear in a way that allows our children to feel hopeful when they dream of their futures? If we are serious, if there is to be a call to arms, the form this action should take, the one which will serve humanity best must be spiritual in nature, again, not religious. In my youth, there was a movement known as the "Age of Aquarius."[99] It spoke of "that time when humanity would take control of the Earth and its own destiny as its rightful heritage, with humanity's destiny being the revelation of truth and the expansion of consciousness."[100] For this movement to succeed, it will take action on the part of all of us. Perhaps it is time to revisit the movement that failed to materialize during my youth, for those of today's youth. Since Renaissance times, we have lived in a material world, driven to a place where humanity's inequality is staggering, and the future is in need of a light to pierce its darkness.

Everything I've shared is old news, it's known to all whether acknowledged or whether ignored. With this information having been disseminated for nearly a decade, no actions have yet been taken. To address the fears of a great nation will require great sacrifice. At the end of this soliloquy should these words fall upon deaf ears, all shall not be lost. It is my intention to leave an answer for our youth, one I have taken action to create. Fear not, and let us continue.

Chapter Eleven

A SOCIAL CONTRACT BROKEN

'm not going on a witch-hunt; suffice it to say over the past couple of centuries, the science of physics from a material perspective has not benefitted the citizenry of our nation. With the greatest generation, they had survived the Great Depression. A depression caused by embracing a business model that made America great for only a few rather than the many. In 1995, the reins of financial power were passed on from one generation to the next. Where the experience of the Great Depression had made the Greatest Generation an excellent financial steward, the generation of Boomers that followed had different experiences we'd drawn from. In the 1970s a CEO's pay was twenty times the typical workers' pay. In 1980, that rose to 42-to-1, and in the 2000s pay rose once again to 120-to-1. Today, the average CEO pay has been adjusted to 344-to-1.

In 2008, the Baby Boomers, who had been in charge for just over a decade, triggered the Great Recession worldwide. Due to the subprime mortgage crisis they created, all generations had to bail out the bankers. As a result, Generation X experienced the financial strains of the Great Recession, seen as pressures of caring for both children and aging parents. Along with increased cost of living, property depreciation, sky-high rent, student loan debt, and job insecurity.

The Millennials were also hit hard by financial struggles. They earned less, worked longer, received fewer benefits, and faced a scarcity of stable, well-paying, full-time jobs. A social contract was broken, raising concerns that this generation would not reach the same financial stability their parents had achieved.

For Generation Z the material world has revealed its immoral side in the form of Global Warming. The material business model, driven to make every ounce count, has finally shown its true worth. We are now on the brink of financial, physical, mental, emotional, and spiritual bankruptcy.

The basis of the material model and the underlying science are in need of significant change. Much more could be said but words are no longer adequate. As a nation, it is time we come together and consider our youth in determining if we should take a stand. I know how capable we as a people are, I'm just not sure there's a willingness to do what's right.

I have long contemplated how I can make a positive impact on the youth I have dedicated my life to. As we move further into the 21st century, I am committed to changing the current trajectory we're on. Should there be a lack of community in taking a stand, so be it. I clearly possess what is essential to succeed, alone if necessary. That's a vision conceived, a heart that believes, and the passion to achieve. I now present for rigorous review "Honor Bound Academy, Inc.,"[101] a 501(c) 3 organization. As its "Adolescent Combat Diplomate," I have created a one-of-a-kind "Rite of Passage,"[102] program for adolescents transitioning into adulthood at the ages of eighteen, nineteen, and twenty. Please let me share what this entails.

In order to define "Honor Bound Academy"[103] I'll use Patrons, geographic locations, Native American participation, for visualization with HBA's architectural descriptions of various Citadels referenced in J.R.R. Tolkien's masterpiece, *The Silmarillion*,[104] along with an inclusion of several attachments: the Executive Summary, Strategic Vision, and Budget. I, too, would like to offer further observations, which I believe to be pertinent. These observations are meant for those who believe in magic, those who look at this world of ours through eyes that behold all that is amazing, and all who still look up at the stars with awe and wonder.

I've written this soliloquy as a vehicle to share the "Rite of Passage,"[105] creating it for those who are the same age I was when I experienced mine. This is not the only reason; I also want to address the American people regarding our current interactions with one another in light of the upcoming election of the next President of the United States. As it stands, we are moving towards a convergence that leaves us vulnerable, with the potential of losing much, if not all, that we cherish.

America, I have long observed the behaviors and actions of an honorable people. I too, have observed the world at large along with their behaviors and actions. With the eye of a clinical therapist (LCSW) and a Navy SEAL, I see underlying activities occurring that are not readily seen through all the chaos. There are mental health concerns, leading to addiction, homelessness, and a division of friends, families, neighbors, and entire communities. I too, have watched a cadre of Americans whose sole purpose is to attain wealth no matter the cost. Those such as the Sackler family, owners of Purdue Pharma, who are responsible for the emergence of the opioid epidemic. Additionally, even more nefarious are the nation-states that meddle in our affairs. Some of these are foreign countries operating as police states, restricting the freedom and will of their own people as they commit espionage, steal trade secrets, seek to weaken our security architecture, going so far as transporting without concern drugs such as Fentanyl. There are also thug states that have fallen from power after a long Cold War, and they, too, are unleashing their own forms of manipulation upon us by tampering with our sacred trust, such as through the manipulation of our hallowed right to vote.

Can we honestly say that there is a politician in modern day America whom we would want our children to emulate? I can't predict the future, but I can help shape it by writing, as was suggested to our youth, and by taking up the pen to inscribe our own history. We are a charismatic collection of diverse peoples who have been given a precious gift called democracy. This gift requires constant vigilance and the sharing of absolute truth, from those whom we elect, along with a media that informs its citizenry with fact-based truth.

Our leaders are currently feeding us the information they believe we want to hear, regardless of the truth. We are also being manipulated by leaders abroad for their own benefit, as they perceive us as a divided, weak, and pathetic people whose greatness is merely an illusion. Meanwhile, they are mocking us.

Having now unveiled a fair amount of information, I'd like to initiate the primary purpose of this noble endeavor. My intention is to provide solutions to the issues our nation is facing, particularly those affecting our youth. At this point in the soliloquy, I will share the research I have conducted through the creation of my non-profit "Honor Bound Academy, Inc."[106]

Chapter Twelve

BOUND BY HONOR

The saying goes, "We have two ears and one mouth so that we can listen twice as much as we speak."[107] What follows is a product of my imagination: an institution called Honor Bound Academy (HBA)[108] that can and will prepare our youth for a future where they will be supported spiritually, emotionally, and mentally throughout their lives. In the sections to follow, I will lay out my suggestion as a legacy for addressing the issues facing our national treasure, our children.

I've tried but failed to find a funding source. However, I refuse to allow all my dreams for your betterment to end in failure. I'm not giving in, nor am I giving up. Instead, I will share all necessary information with you through the words of this soliloquy, leaving behind the knowledge for individuals, groups, or for future visionaries. I understand that certain aspects of another's version of Honor Bound Academy (HBA)[109] will need to be altered.

Honor Bound Academy[110] is not a singularity. The intention was to place one in every state of the union. I began writing down all the requirements for an HBA[111] during my work as a Military and Family Life Consultant (MFLC—2008). This job required extensive travel within the United States and abroad.

Having lived or served in California, Idaho, Montana, Colorado, Texas, Michigan, Georgia, Florida, South Carolina, North Carolina, and Virginia. I knew that each state, along with the state's population, was unique and original; none of these states are alike. For example, there was no way to create an Honor Bound Academy[112] in California, then recreate every aspect when building in Texas, or Mississippi. This would only lead to disaster.

When I was assigned to work with Special Operations Command (SOCOM) as a Military and Family Life Counselor (MFLC), I had the opportunity to work with a variety of Special Forces groups and operators, including the Green Berets, Rangers (Scroll), Night Stalkers, Raiders, CCT, PJ's, and SR of the Air Force. Without the kind of relationship I experienced, it would not be feasible for another to utilize SF Operators as I would.

I will not tell, suggest, or recommend what individuals or groups will or should do in the future to address these issues, but necessity will play a significant role, as it is the mother of all inventions and fully capable of serving this purpose. Additionally, seeking guidance from Native American counsel in harmony with nature will be a powerful ally, creating the intended outcome. Furthermore, providing hands-on guidance to adolescents as they transition into adulthood by caring individuals is a noble endeavor, one that is "Bound by Honor."

Throughout the process, from start to finish, I've sought to maintain focus, provide clarity when needed, and deliver difficult truths, when necessary, along with hope, faith, and charity. If it weren't for the opportunity to spend time with the youth that has been part of my life, I don't know where I would be today. I am sincerely grateful to all the confidants, guides, and mentors who taught me how to be a trusted adult.

I now present for your evaluation "Honor Bound Academy,"[113] my gift for today's youth.

Chapter 13

HONOR BOUND ACADEMY[114]

Statistics reveal that adolescent males in their late teenage years increasingly need programs that will help to guide them through the confusing labyrinth of transitioning from childhood to adulthood. Crime, alcoholism, and suicide rates continue to either increase or remain a significant problem in American society. We, as a society, are called to act.

One Hundred selected males eighteen to twenty years of age will experience a fully immersive, 365-day program called Honor Bound Academy (HBA)[115] based in Sonoma County, California, where a team consisting of a licensed clinical social worker, volunteer (Special Forces) mentors, and staff will expose these protégé learners to an academic education, nature-filled experiences, and counseling that will dramatically improve their self-esteem and instill in them a sense of honor. *Honor Bound Academy will bestow within each a philosophy that they are honor-bound to themselves, their teammates, and society as a whole.*[116]

In a blog found on my LinkedIn[117] page titled "Adolescent Combat Diplomate," I described the merger of four (4) categories with nine (9) line items in each to tell one (1) story, this story. I plan to do this by creating a total of ten (10) short stories pairing each with:

1. An individual Patron, one of the 11 wealthiest Americans

2. A Special Forces Command

3. A Native American tribe along with its geographical location; and

4. Utilization of J.R.R. Tolkien's middle-earth structural names found in *The Silmarillion*.[118]

All of this to show connectivity through the creation of Honor Bound Academy's,[119] in various presented ensembles (below), throughout America.

WILLIAM "BILL" HENRY GATES:[120] (SAGE)

WARREN EDWARD BUFFETT:[121] (ORACLE)
8492/5326[122]—"SF BAY AREA"—"COMANCHE"[123]—"KHAZAD-DUM"[124]

MICHAEL BLOOMBERG:[125]
NAVY SEAL[126]—"NEW YORK"—"IROQUOIS"[127]—"GONDOLIN"[128]

LAWRENCE "LARRY" JOSEPH ELLISON:[129]
JSOC [130]—"ALASKA"—"INUIT" [131]—"MINAS TIRITH" [132]

PHILIP "PHIL" HAMPSON KNIGHT: [133]
RANGER[134]—"OREGON"—"NEZ PERCE" [135]—"MENEGROTH" [136]

ELON REEVE MUSK: [137]
NIGHT STALKER[138]—"FLORIDA"—"SEMINOLE"[139]—"ISENGARD"[140]

JEFFREY "JEFF" PRESTON BEZOS: [141]
GREEN BERET[142]—"NEW MEXICO"—"NAVAJO" [143]—"IMLADRIS"[144]

CARL CELIAN ICAHN: [145]
MARSOC[146]—"VIRGINIA"—"CHEROKEE"[147]—"BELEGOST"[148]

MARK ELLIOT ZUCKERBERG: [149]
PJ[150]—"SOUTH DAKOTA"—"LAKOTA SIOUX"[151]—"NOGROD"[152]

LAWRENCE "LARRY" EDWARD PAGE: [153]
CCT[154]—"MICHIGAN"—"OTTAWA AND CHIPPEWA"[155]—"NARGOTHROND"[156]

SERGEY MIKHAILOVICH BRIN:[157]
SR[158]—"MISSISSIPPI"—"NATCHEZ"[159]—"GREY HAVENS"[160]

Honor Bound Academy is organized into the above nine (9) groups, including the group formed by the Oracle, Sage, and myself, the Adolescent Combat Diplomate (8492/5326)[161], making a total of ten (10) groups. Each group is located in the geographical area of the specific Native American tribe representing each Honor Bound Academy (HBA).[162] For Khazad-Dum,[163] the connection is with the Comanche[164] Nation and the location will be Northern California (SF Bay Area). The reason is simple: I was born and raised in this area. If I'm going to ask the people of this nation to have faith in this program, it's only right that I start it in my own backyard.

KHAZAD-DUM PART[165] — I

William "Bill" Henry Gates:[166] *(SAGE)*

Warren Edward Buffett:[167] *(ORACLE)*

8492/5326[168]—"SF BAY AREA"—"COMANCHE"[169]—"KHAZAD-DUM"[170]

I had a lucid dream that felt astonishingly real, with colors so incredibly vivid. What made it wonderful was the awareness that I knew I was dreaming. I have had this dream countless times during waking hours. It always starts the same way—four of us sitting at a table, playing a game of bridge. My partner and I are facing off against the Oracle and the Sage. These are the names I've given to the two adversaries, Warren Buffett, and Bill Gates, whom we face every time we play.

The dream continues to evolve as my consciousness leads us on a journey, which remains the same journey regardless of when I have this experience. Alongside me is my holy man, my shaman, my spiritual guide, or, in simple terms, my bridge-playing partner. The four of us share a common denominator of ruthlessness. The Oracle and Sage demonstrate this in their business dealings, while my shaman embraces a system ingrained in the belief that "if it cannot be both," a leader should be feared rather than loved. As for me, my ruthlessness comes from my background as a (rootin, tootin, lootin, parashootin, double-cap crimpin) frogman. Despite our shared ruthlessness, it is important to note that we all possess admirable virtues at our core.

This lucid dream, whether waking or sleeping, allows me to guide the four of us onward, downward from the eastern gate of Khazad-Dum,[171] across Durin's bridge,[172] and on into the Chamber of Mazarbul.[173] Why Khazad-Dum?[174] Why the Chamber of Mazarbul (which means the Chamber of Records)? [175] The reason why is because this dream I share with you is my dream. The dream that one day, the Honor Bound Academy, Inc.,[176] my 501 (C) 3 will be a reality rather than a dream that exists only in my imagination.

In the previous article titled "Adolescent Combat Diplomate," I described the merger of four (4) categories with nine (9) line items in each to tell one (1) story; this one. I plan to do this in a total of ten (10) short stories found with:

1. An individual Patron, one of the eleven wealthiest Americans

2. A Special Forces Command; and

3. A Native American tribe, along with its geographical location

4. Utilization of J. R. R. Tolkien's Middle-earth Citadel's.

All of this is to outline the creation of Honor Bound Academies[177] through various presented ensembles.

As we fall back into the dream, here we find ourselves in the Chamber of Records.[178] The four of us are witnessing the unfolding of America's newly created "Rite of Passage,"[179] for our eighteen, nineteen, and twenty-year-old citizens as they transition from adolescence to adulthood. Imagine digging a hole 300 yards deep, then building a vast fortress measuring 300 yards wide and 300 yards in length. Once it is completed, we would bury it, creating an underground Academy similar to the way the manor of the Naugrim or dwarves did. Their history can be found in *The Silmarillion*[180] and will be taught as part of the education at our Honor Bound Academy,[181] known as Khazad-Dum[182] (Honor Bound Academy[183]).

As the dream continues, we four find ourselves encountering the Guardians of Khazad-Dum.[184] These elders belong to the Comanche Tribe; in the past, these spiritual guides were characterized as the "Lords of the Plains."[185] Comanche power relied on bison, horses, trading, and raiding. The horse played a crucial role in the emergence of a distinctive Comanche culture; "the band was the primary social unit of the Comanche. A typical band might number several hundred people."[186]

"The Comanche looked on the children as their most precious gift."[187] Doing so as the boys grew older, they were encouraged to be skillful hunters "as they learned to patiently and quietly stalk game. They became more self-reliant . . . by playing together as a group, also formed the bonds and cooperative spirit that they would need when they hunted and raided."[188] Most importantly, the teaching of their language by spiritual leaders was crucial. The merging of the horse, hunting, and language created a unique, self-sustaining culture for the Dwarrowdelf[189] of this Honor Bound Academy.[190]

I have extensive experience in navigating the various programs at the Honor Bound Academies[191], particularly the Special Forces Training Command at Khazad-Dum[192]. I have successfully completed BUD/S and have a thorough understanding of each of the nine specific SF schools; during five of the seven years I worked as a Military and Family Life Counselor (MFLC), I worked with each of them.

I awaken to the recurrent dream described above each time with a feeling of fraternity, solidarity, harmony, camaraderie, and Esprit de corps. This is a brotherhood; each Honor Bound Academy[193] will be offered to a generation of our youth, all deserving to experience this awesome feeling.

KHAZAD-DUM[194] PART – II

William "Bill" Henry Gates:[195] (SAGE)

Warren Edward Buffett:[196] (ORACLE)

8492/5326[197] — "SF BAY AREA" — "COMMANCHE"[198] — "KHAZAD-DUM"[199]

Why choose Warren Buffett as The Oracle and Bill Gates as The Sage? I've spent the last thirty-plus years preparing for this opportunity, educating myself through colleges and universities, along with years of amassing numerous continuing educational units. I've always held myself to the highest expectations, and throughout my journey, I have been selective about who I allow to teach, mentor, or counsel me. I am excited to share with you the creation of Honor Bound Academy (HBA)[200]. This started with my first and most important educational component, Basic Underwater Demolition / SEAL (BUD/S) training. Throughout my military career, I received education from only the highest caliber individuals. Naturally, when it comes to the Patrons, I have sought to pair with only the best. That pertains to the various Native American tribes, Special Forces operatives, and middle-earth structures. Nine (9) individual combinations of Patrons are used as an example in telling the stories, along with one pair of Patrons for me.

My patrons, the Oracle, and the Sage, are the first of the eleven wealthiest men in America. They have achieved their station in life by surrounding themselves with only the best, just as I have done. Mr. Buffett and Mr. Gates are crucial in shaping Honor Bound Academy[201] so that it provides our youth with the opportunity to make a profound impact on themselves and our nation as a whole.

When all ten (10) Honor Bound Academies[202] are up and running, the crucial requirement is for each of the ten (10) to be the same, with no two being identical. A contradiction? Not really. This truth is based on my association with Navy SEALs worldwide, our sense of brotherhood, and our community that understands that while we are all the same, and no two of us are alike is common-speak.

For clarity, let me explain what defines a Navy SEAL from all others. It is our ability to shoot, move, and communicate. Our greatest asset is the ability to communicate effectively while operating. This allows us to move as a cohesive unit, in singularity, regardless of our numbers. This is our greatest asset, and it is what makes us truly special. The gift and distinction of being trained as a Navy SEAL set me apart from others who offer programs to our youth. My ability to connect and unite them for the greater good of our nation, is what makes me uniquely qualified.

GONDOLIN[203]

Michael Bloomberg:[204]

NAVY SEAL[205] — "NEW YORK" — "IROQUOIS"[206] — "GONDOLIN"[207]

I've begun sharing the various Honor Bound Academy[208] levels from one (1) through ten (10). I began with the first two patrons, "The Oracle and the Sage." I then described the Special Forces knowledge based on my own military experience both as an Operator and DOD contractor. Next, I discussed the leadership or spiritual center from a Native American perspective (Comanche), followed by the living structure described as the ancient dwarf mansion known as Khazad-Dum. [209]

For the second iteration of the Honor Bound Academy, its physical location will change to upstate New York. There, the spiritual guides will come from the Iroquois people. This (HBA)[210] will be situated in a secluded Valley surrounded by tall mountains, within a hidden fortress named Gondolin,[211] also known as Ondolinde (The Rock of the Music of Water). Its patron is Michael Ruben Bloomberg. The Special Forces mentors will come from the ranks of the Navy SEALs.

I believe that our surroundings shape who we are. This is why it is so important for our young protégé learners to be surrounded only by the best. I want them to wake up each day in a magical realm, with a 360-degree awe-inspiring presence, and to receive the best administration for their unique HBAs[212] education. Building Gondolin,[213] in the real world is inspired by J.R.R. Tolkien's *The Silmarillion*.[214] In his mythological fantasy, it had seven names, with Ondolinde[215] being the first one shared. It was also known as Gar Thurion (Secret Place),[216] Gondolbar (City of Stone),[217] Gondothlimbar (City of the Dwellers in Stone),[218] Gwarestrin (Tower of the Guard),[219] Gondost (Stone Fortress),[220] which was described as one of the most stunning pieces of construction in all of middle-earth.

The location is important, but so is the Patron, Michael Bloomberg. He is an American businessman, politician, philanthropist, and author who served as the mayor of New York City and ran for president. He has established public charter schools, improved urban infrastructure, supported public health initiatives, and introduced environmental protections. Education is crucial to the Honor Bound Academy[221] just as it has been for Gondolin's[222] Patron, Mr. Bloomberg. His journey began with achieving Eagle Scout status and degrees in Electrical Engineering and an MBA from John Hopkins University and Harvard Business School, respectively.

The Iroquois, later known as the Six Nations, are spiritually at the center. Out of respect and to clarify, I present the name Haudenosaunee (meaning "People of the Longhouse")[223], since some scholars consider the name "Iroquois" to be derogatory. Regardless, the mythology found amongst Native American tribes has much to teach, including creation stories and folktales. In each village, there was a storyteller who was responsible for learning all the stories by heart, such as Ga-oh, the personification of the wind, and So-son-do-wah, the great hunter. Dreams also played a significant role in spirituality, as seen through ceremonies addressing nature such as farming, healing, thanksgiving, and condolence ceremonies after death.

The mentoring corps for upstate New York's Academy, Gondolin,[224] whose patron is Michael Bloomberg, will be enhanced with instruction from Navy SEALs, and spiritual leadership from the Haudenosaunee people. Honor Bound Academy, regardless of its name or geographical location, will have the same curriculum. The difference will be in the perspective of the mentors, in this case, the SEAL instructors.

What sets SEALs apart from other SF Operators is their use of water. Water is a powerful element in their training program, evoking a wide range of emotions from pure joy to primal fear. A smaller version of the Navy SEALs' BUD/S "Hell Week," this training exercise teaches students that they can surpass their self-imposed limits. Over a 72-hour period without sleep, students face physical, emotional, and intellectual challenges. They endure being cold, wet, and miserable but come to realize that they possess a reserve of self-reliance, toughness, and resiliency that is stronger than they ever imagined.

It is all about "we" not "me". The connection between individuals is a gift that everyone will cherish forever. In this case, the combination of Mr. Michael Bloomberg along with Gondolin[225] as the academy site, supported through "The People of the Longhouse,"[226] and taught by UDT/SEAL operators is priceless.

With my current beliefs, I can envision an Honor Bound Academy[227] in every state of the union. To expedite this, I will now describe eight (8) more times how each independent Honor Bound Academy[228] will unfold across America. Regardless of the challenges the youth may face at an HBA,[229] they will all come to understand that they are not alone.

MINAS TIRITH[230]

Lawrence "Larry" Joseph Ellison:[231]

JSOC[232] — "ALASKA" — "INUIT"[233] — "MINAS TIRITH"[234]

For the third Honor Bound Academy (HBA),[235] it will be Minas Anor, more commonly known as Minas Tirith,[236] one of the most astounding pieces of architecture that will be built by men, for men, and for our young men. Its name is translated as the "Tower of the Setting Sun,"[237] and for the latter, it is translated as the "Tower of the Guard."[238]

The patron of this Honor Bound Academy[239] is Lawrence Joseph 'Larry' Ellison,[240] an American business magnate, investor, and philanthropist who is a co-founder, Executive Chairman, and Chief Technology Officer of Oracle Corporation. The spiritual support for this HBA[241] comes from the Inuit,[242] the Native American tribe inhabiting Alaska's Arctic region. Instructors will be drawn from the Joint Special Operations Command (JSOC).[243]

This matching of unique cultural partners at each level creates a powerful fusion of talent. Across Inuit[244] cultures, oral traditions recount past feats, including conflicts with other indigenous groups. Historical records of violence against outsiders indicate a history of hostile encounters within Inuit[245] cultures and with other societies. In terms of justice within the Inuit[246] culture, governance granted significant authority to the elders, serving as a key moderating influence. Inuit[247] spiritualism is closely linked to a system of rituals that are integrated into the daily life of the people. According to a customary Inuit[248] belief, "the harshness and unpredictability of life in the Arctic ensured that the Inuit lived with concern for the uncontrollable. A streak of bad luck could destroy an entire community."[249] These rituals were simple yet considered necessary.

To filter through the paradigm of uncontrollability, the choice of Lawrence Ellison and JSOC[250] is appropriate when it comes to matching certain distinctive personality types of youth found in sufficient numbers across our country. As for Mr. Lawrence 'Larry' Ellison, his journey began in 1966 at the age of twenty-two, having made a trip from Chicago to California in a flashy turquoise Thunderbird. By 1977, he had co-founded Software Development Laboratories, which ultimately became Oracle Systems Corporation, in 1982. Mr. Ellison embodies the typical characteristics of a brash Apex operator, displaying essential ruthlessness. He is notorious for disparaging competitors and utilizing his substantial wealth in various impactful ways, such as investing in the educational platform maker, Leapfrog Enterprises. Additionally, he has a reputation for extravagant spending over the years. The key element regarding Mr. Lawrence Joseph Ellison is the simple fact that no matter what he says, he has always backed it up with actionable deeds.

When asked why he had to win the Americas Cup Yacht race twice, he described a personality that would not allow him to quit while losing, which he had done prior to winning. Then after winning the cup, that same personality did not allow for quitting while winning. This may not make sense to everyone, but (JSOC)[251] operators, Mr. Ellison, and a certain type of red-blooded American youth, all to be housed in the mysterious realm of Minas Tirith,[252] it makes perfect sense.

Across this nation, our youth possess special and unique abilities, but far too many will never live up to their abilities due to a random fate or a lack of opportunity, which is not only a shame but unacceptable. I have worked as a social worker for several decades, primarily with individuals living on the fringes of our society. In this place, opportunity is a tricky proposition, especially for youth who find themselves on the fringes simply by chance. The vision I possess seeks to bring a counterbalance to a well-thought-out opportunity (HBA).[253] I have stated, "You are as your surroundings dictate," in this case, a pairing of surreal companions. The Joint Special Operations Command (JSOC)[254] was formed by selecting the top candidates from the East and West Coast Seal Teams, including seventy-six original members of SEAL Team Six (Task Force Blue)[255] of which there were 76 original Apex pupils, (later known as DEVGROUP).[256] Regarding Honor Bound Academy (HBA),[257] in the form of Minas Tirith,[258] there will always be a need for a finishing school, for those born with innate skills.

Out of the (9), nine other Academies there will be hidden gems scattered throughout the ranks. To train these special individuals, Mentors with their own fully developed talents are required. These individuals wear various shades on their uniforms (JSOC).[259] Their talents are diverse, coming from the Sea, Air, and Land. The individuals who are like brothers from different mothers, and like the Patron Mr. Ellison of Minas Tirith[260] located in Alaska's Arctic zone, are expected to demonstrate a history of proven actions.

Mythology: Joseph Campbell once said that we are unable to create modern myths. He said these times we live in change too quickly from day to week, to month, and so on throughout the years. He believes that we do not have a mythology that can keep up with the rapid changes in our lives. He also pointed out that new powers are being revealed to us through the capabilities of machines, stating "We cannot have a mythology for a long, long time to come; things are changing too fast. The environment in which we are living is changing too fast for it to become mythologized."[261] I wish Joseph Campbell were here to see what we're about to attempt. Although he no longer lives, this challenge is worthy, especially with me, our patrons, Native Americans, Special Forces mentors, and specifically today's youth. For them, it is a fact that tomorrow is never going to get here, and time is always oh-so slow.

MENEGROTH[262]

Philip "Phil" Hampson Knight:[263]

RANGER[264] — "OREGON" — "NEZ PERCE"[265] — "MENEGROTH"[266]

We now come to the fourth (4) Honor Bound Academy (HBA),[267] "Menegroth, Menegroth the fair and Menegroth the great, Menegroth the thousand caves they call it."[268] It will undoubtedly be an engineering marvel. Where Khazad-Dum[269] was built by digging a hole, creating a structure, and then burying it, Menegroth[270] will be different. Dispersed throughout the state of Oregon are sprawling systems of caves. Some run for several dark miles just beneath the desert floor, while others have skylights opening up to the light of day.

The Patron of Menegroth[271] is a native Oregonian. An American business magnate and philanthropist, Philip "Phil" Hampson Knight[272] is a co-founder and current chairman emeritus of Nike, Inc. He earned his journalism degree from the University of Oregon. Immediately after graduating, Mr. Knight enlisted in the Army and served one year on active duty and seven years in the Army Reserve. He then enrolled at Stanford Graduate School of Business. What makes Philip Knight rare is his athleticism. As a middle-distance runner, his best time at one (1) mile is 4 minutes, 10 seconds, making him world-class and perfect to blend in with the Nez Perce.[273]

The name, Nez Perce,[274] was popularized by French explorers and trappers. The Nez Perce people refer to themselves as "Nimiipuu," which means "the walking people" or "we, the people,"[275] in their own language. "Their mythology and sacred concepts revolve around a "Great Spirit," which forms the basis of Native American beliefs. While some tribes believed in multiple deities, the Nez Perce held their own mythology in high regard. The "Great Spirit" was seen with every wind; seen in every cloud, feared in sounds, and adored in every place that inspires awe. While cultures and customs varied among tribes, they all believed that the universe was bound together by spirits of natural life. These strong and spirited people managed to keep their many legends and stories alive. Passed down through the generations, these many tales speak of timeless messages of peace, life, death, and harmony with nature."[276]

For this segment, I will introduce a merging of the Special Forces Operators assigned to Patron Philip Hampson 'Phil' Knight,[277] including the Nez Perce[278] and Menegroth[279] who are being mentored by instructors of the United States Army Rangers.[280] History is incredibly important; remembering it, or more importantly, making it, is paramount. "The earliest mention of Ranger operations comes from Captain John "Samuel" Smith," who wrote in 1622: "When I had ten men able to go abroad, our commonwealth was very strong. With such a number, I ranged that unknown country 14 weeks."[281] The term range, ranging, and ranger were frequently used, as in "The American Ranger had been born."[282] "The father of American Ranging is Colonel Benjamin Church (1639–1718).[283] At the time, he was a Captain, and he "designed his force primarily to emulate Native American patterns of war. He learned to fight like Native Americans from Native Americans. Americans became rangers exclusively under the tutelage of the Native American allies. Rangers depended on Native Americans as both allies and teachers.[284]

This is where we can see that history does, can, and will often repeat itself. Regarding the previous realms (Khazad-Dum,[285] Gondolin,[286]and Minas Tirith), this Honor Bound Academy (HBA)[287] of Menegroth,[288] along with the seven other HBA's[289] to come, will merge a Patron, a Tolkien Citadel, the Special Forces unit, along with the natural harmonizing myths and sacred ways of the Native Americans, also known as the original or first Americans.

ISENGARD[290]

Elon Reeve Musk:[291]

NIGHT STALKER[292] — "FLORIDA" — "SEMINOLE"[293] — "ISENGARD"[294]

The fifth (5) Honor Bound Academy (HBA)[295] will be named Isengard,[296] also known as Orthanc,[297] which in Tolkien's mythological world is one of Numenorean[298] construct. It is an example of the classical wonders of Middle Earth. It's a marvel in its construction, a wonder in its material, and a sight to behold. For our purposes, it will be created using granite, as a circular pillar 100 feet at its base, reaching toward the heavens at a grand total of 555 feet. On the exterior, each class logo, including words, will be chiseled in ascending relief, starting with the first class. Each relief measures 3 feet by 5 feet — a depicted personal representation that numerically winds its way from the bottom to the very top. Its geographical location will be on the East Coast in the state of Florida, surrounding the pinnacle tower of Isengard[299]

A ring of rocks with a single gate as the southern entrance will be built between a set of prominent hills. Upon closer observation, the rocks reveal sleeping quarters, classrooms, and administration offices blended in such a way that they do not look like any construction of Men but the product of time on the upheaval of the hills themselves.

The Patron of Isengard[300] is Elon Reeve Musk,[301] an engineer, industrial designer, technology entrepreneur, and philanthropist. He is the founder, CEO, and chief engineer/designer of Space X; early investor, CEO, and product architect of Tesla, Inc.; founder of the Boring Company; co-founder of Neuralink; and co-founder and initial co-chairman of OpenAI. It is astonishing, to think of the potential when a visionary such as this merges and embraces a code of conduct allowing HBA[302] and its youth to take a set of actions that are likely to prolong civilization, minimize the probability of a dark age, and reduce the length of a dark age, if indeed one should emerge in the real world. Furthermore, Mr. Musk is the type of Patron that makes you wonder. If there is any doubt that the Honor Bound Academies[303] are possible, Elon Reeve Musk[304] is a living testimony to what is possible.

As a counterbalance to the extraordinary structure of Isengard,[305] its Patron, Mr. Elon Reeve Musk,[306] we include support for the spiritual well-being of the original people of Florida, known as the Seminoles.[307] "The word "Seminole"[308] comes from the Muskogee (Creeks) word *simano-li*, which has been translated as "frontiersmen," "outcast," "runaway," "separatist," and similar words."[309] More speculatively, the Creek word itself "may itself be derived from the Spanish word *cimarion*, meaning "runaway," or "wild-one."[310] The "Seminole[311] tribes" have a unique spiritual aspect and have assimilated escaped slaves from the Southern States at various times in their history.

The Seminoles of Florida are known for their strength and resistance against the United States to maintain their independence and sovereignty over their lands and traditional way of life. In the latter part of the 20th century (1970, 1980, and 1990), concerns about the loss of land, language, and traditions led to a revival of old crafts and traditional culture.

Around the same time and half a world away "Operation Eagle Claw,"[312] was unfolding in an attempt to rescue American hostages held in Tehran, Iran. The Night Stalkers[313] were formed after the botched attempt to rescue these hostages from the U.S. Embassy, where eight (8) service members gave their lives. "The 160th Special Operations Aviation Regiment (Airborne) abbreviated as 160th SOAR (A), is a special operations force of the United States Army that provides helicopter aviation support for general purpose forces and special operation forces."[314] "Its missions have included attack, assault, and reconnaissance, and these missions are usually conducted at night, at high speeds, low altitudes, and on short notice."[315] "Nicknamed the Night Stalkers, the 160th SOAR (A) consists of the Army's best-qualified aviators, crew chiefs, and support soldiers. Upon joining the 160th, all soldiers are assigned to "Green Platoon," where they receive intensive training in 'advanced methods of the five basic combat skills: first responder, land navigation, combative, weapons, and teamwork.'"[316]

Crucial to all (HBA's)[317] is teamwork. The construction of Isengard,[318] its Patron Elon Reeve Musk,[319] and the spiritual culture presented through the Seminoles[320] or "Free People,"[321] and a mentoring staff consisting of 160th SOAR (A) Night Stalkers,[322] who don't quit, are essential and will create magic, mystery, and miracles.

IMLADRIS[323]

Jeffrey "Jeff" Preston Bezos:[324]

GREEN BERET[325] — "NEW
MEXICO" — "NAVAJO"[326] — "IMLADRIS"[327]

Our journey continues as we arrive at the sixth (6) Honor Bound Academy (HBA).[328] This name may be familiar to readers and moviegoers of "The Hobbit" and "The Lord of the Rings." Imladris[329] is better known as "The Last Homely House East of the Sea," or Rivendell.[330] It is described as the domain of Elrond half-elven. According to John Ronald Reuel Tolkien (J.R.R.T), it was established in 1967 in the Second Age and lasted until the end of the Third Age. According to our Tolkien enthusiasts, it resembles the "Celtic Otherworld of Tir na nOg."[331] In real life, the Valley of Imladris, where Rivendell is situated,[332] is based on the modern-day landscape of Lauterbrunnen, Switzerland.

Little is left to the imagination when you can actually observe this in its authentic geography. However, for an Honor Bound Academy,[333] you need to have a large hall for feasting, other halls for berthing, and numerous classrooms for learning. Additionally, there should be a separate hall, called the Hall of Fire,[334] where a fire will burn year-round with carved pillars on either side of the hearth. This space will be used for singing and storytelling.

The valley where Imladris[335] will be created is in "The Land of Enchantment,"[336] also known simply as the state of New Mexico.[337]

The patron for Imladris[338] is Jeffrey "Jeff" Preston Bezos,[339] who, among many things, was the valedictorian of his high school graduation class. In his speech, he told his high school peers that he dreamed of the day mankind would colonize space. This early vision of a visionary turned out to be an authentic visualization. Regarding his higher education, Jeffrey "Jeff" Bezos graduated from Princeton with a Bachelor of Science in Engineering and Computer Science. In addition to founding Blue Origin, a human spaceflight startup company, he also acquired "The Washington Post,"[340] and was one of the first shareholders of Google. What truly sets Jeffrey "Jeff" Preston Bezos[341] apart as a one-of-a-kind Patron can be summed up in one word, "Amazon." The decision was made to establish an online bookstore. He left his position at the age of thirty, having attained a senior vice president position at a hedge fund. He then founded Amazon, literally in his garage. Ultimately, Mr. Jeffrey "Jeff" Preston Bezos,[342] in a period of twenty-five years (1993–2018), would go on to become officially the wealthiest man alive.

To establish a spiritual foundation, it is essential to introduce Native American culture. To achieve this, the Navajo Nation[343], its people, and the territory covering parts of northeastern Arizona, northeastern New Mexico, and a small portion of Utah have been selected. The Honor Bound Academy (HBA),[344] will be located within a valley in the state of New Mexico.[345]

During World War II, the Navajo[346] people played a significant role as Code-talkers. Approximately 400 to 500 Native Americans in the United States Marine Corps were tasked with transmitting secret tactical messages. The Navajo[347] language, with its complex grammar, was not mutually intelligible with even its closest relatives and was still unwritten at the time of WWII. The official designation of the word "Navajo"[348] and the people's tradition of governance are rooted in their clan and oral history. The Navajo people have a system of rules of behavior that extends to a refined culture that the Navajo[349] people acknowledge as "walking in beauty."[350] The philosophy and clan system were established long before the colonial occupation of "Dinetah,"[351] the term used for the traditional homeland of the Navajo.[352]

To bring the final component into account, a powerful, unique, connection is established with the introduction of the Green Beret.[353] Through assimilation, Mr. Jeffrey "Jeff" Preston Bezos,[354] Imladris,[355] and the United States Army Special Forces, commonly known as the Green Berets,[356] form a mystical fusion. This remarkable union takes advantage of the inherent nature of the Green Berets,[357] who are designed and deployed to carry out nine doctrinal missions: "unconventional warfare, foreign internal defense, direct action, counter-insurgency, special reconnaissance, counter-terrorism, information operations, counter-proliferation of weapons of mass destruction, and security force assistance, through seven geographically focused groups."[358] The first two missions "emphasize language, cultural, and training skills in working with foreign troops."[359] It is this exceptional ability that brings together Imladris,[360] Mr. Jeffrey "Jeff" Preston Bezos,[361] the spiritual foundation of the Navajo,[362] and an instructor corps comprising former Green Beret[363] mentors, approaching a state of enlightenment.

BELEGOST[364]

Carl Celian Icahn:[365]

MARSOC[366] — "VIRGINIA" — "CHEROKEE"[367] — "BELEGOST"[368]

Let's discuss the Seventh (7th) Honor Bound Academy (HBA)[369] named Belegost.[370] In Tolkien's depiction, it was one of the seven (7) great kingdoms of the dwarves (Naugrim).[371] Along with her sister realm, Nogrod,[372] Belegost [373]was located deep beneath Mount Dolmed[374] in the "Blue Mountains in the Ages of Stars." [375] Among the Naugrim (Dwarves) of Belegost[376] were the finest smiths and stone carvers in Middle-Earth. In their armorer's halls they made bright weapons and were the first people to forge chain mail, furthermore these Naugrim [377]carved the stone chambers of Menegroth.[378] An example from *The Silmarillion*[379] shows how the Honor Bound Academies[380] of modern America will cross educate, train, and bond with their sister Academies. This the seventh Honor Bound Academy (HBA)[381] will be found in the state of Virginia buried deep within the Appalachian Mountain range.

The Patron of Belegost[382] is Carl Celian Icahn,[383] old school through and through. In order to understand Mr. Icahn[384] terms like "Corporate Raider,"[385] along with "Hostile Takeover,"[386] need to be clearly defined. In addition, I'll use the definition of ruthless to help clarify.

"Ruthless can be defined as "without ruth" or "having no ruth." So, what then is ruth? The noun ruth, which is now considerably less common than ruthless, means "compassion for the misery of another," "sorrow for one's own faults," or "remorse." And, just as it is possible for one to be without ruth, it is also possible to be full of ruth. The antonym of ruthless is ruthful, meaning "full of ruth" or "tender." Ruthful can also mean "full of sorrow" or "causing sorrow." Ruth can be traced to the middle English noun ruthe, itself from ruen, meaning "to rue" or "to feel regret, remorse, or sorrow."[387]

Bringing together the spiritual foundation with Mr. Carl Icahn[388] and Tolkien's Belegost[389] involves looking into the distant past, specifically, the late 16th Century, where we find the Native American Nation of "The Cherokee,"[390] who occupied the mountain valleys of southwest Virginia. The early Native American history intersects with early American history through Pocahontas, a Powhatan Native American woman known for her involvement with the English colonial settlement at Jamestown, Virginia. Born around 1596, Pocahontas was named Amonute at birth and went by the name Matoaka. She supposedly earned the nickname Pocahontas, which means "playful one," because of her happy inquisitive nature.

From early America of the Cherokee,[391] along with Mr. Carl Icahn,[392] to the most recent accumulation of Special Forces Operators for the US Marine Corps,[393] is the story of Critical Skills Operators (CSO), now known as the Marine Raiders.[394] Special Operations Command (SOCOM)[395] was formed on April 16, 1987, and Marine Special Operations Command (MARSOC)[396] stood up on February 24, 2006.

On 6 August 2014, MARSOC officially bestowed the prestigious "Marine Raider" title upon their subordinate combat unit, the Marine Special Operations Regiment, in honor of the legendary and elite amphibious light infantry unit that operated during World War II.[397] Though this is the youngest of the Special Forces units, its uniqueness can be understood in two simple statements. They are "once a Marine always a Marine," and "all Marines are riflemen." I do not write these words to the many, but to the few, the proud. Yes! I write them as a Navy SEAL, and the only Naval personnel that can talk smack to a Marine and get away with it. Not because I'm a Navy SEAL, but because I am a Naval Hospital Corpsmen "Doc," Hooyah, Semper Fi, 8492/5326.[398]

In closing, this grouping is as unique as the six previous groups of the Honor Bound Academies (HBA)[399]. The pairing of each individual is well thought out, as can be seen here with Mr. Carl Icahn[400] the "Corporate Raider," and "MARSOC—Marine Raider,"[401] a combination that will write its own astonishing history.

NOGROD[402]

Mark Elliot Zuckerberg:[403]

PJ[404]—"SOUTH DAKOTA"—"LAKOTA SIOUX"[405]— "NOGROD"[406]

The sister city to Belegost[407] and the 8th Honor Bound Academy[408] is given the name, Nogrod.[409] According to *The Silmarillion*,[410] "the city was built sometime during the "Years of the Trees," when the western fathers of the Dwarves (Naugrim) awoke from beneath the Ered Luin,"[411] mountain range. It was said that "Nogrod traded throughout Beleriand and the Naugrim were employed for delving and crafts, most famously the Nauglamir.[412] "At the end of the First Age, Nogrod was ruined in the War of Wrath."[413] For the location of Nogrod,[414] the choice is the undisputed queen of maze caves which are found in the Black Hills of South Dakota.

The chosen Patron for this endeavor is an American internet entrepreneur and philanthropist. He is known for co-founding Facebook, Inc. (now known as META), and is as unique as all the other Patrons. He is none other than Mark Elliot Zuckerberg.[415] Additionally, he serves as the chairman and chief executive officer, and is the co-founder of the solar sail spacecraft development project "Breakthrough Starshot."[416]

Generationally, Mark Elliot Zuckerberg[417] is closer in age to those he will serve, which allows him to present from a specific perspective. Not that long ago, he clearly thought of himself as a "hacker" [418] with a motto that said: "it's OK to break things to make them better."[419]

We've all heard the drawbacks of Mr. Mark Elliot Zuckerberg's[420] Facebook, such as privacy concerns, time consumption, and its addictive nature. There is also the issue of it replacing in-person interactions. These concerns apply to much of the technology in today's world. That's why HBA[421] aims to provide a counter-balance by incorporating spiritual practices from ancient American cultures, considering the big picture. In this instance, joining Mr. Mark Elliot Zuckerberg[422] and the state of South Dakota will be the Lakota Sioux[423] of the Black Hills.

"Historically, the Lakota[424] relied on a rich oral tradition to preserve the legends and stories that maintained their spiritual way of life. Elders shared the key values with the youngsters, such as generosity, which in this case means contributing to the betterment of the people. Other such values are those of kinship, wisdom, honesty, humility, and respect. But truly crucial is the value of believing in yourself and facing the challenges that come your way with strength, confidence, and courage. It also includes accepting the problems you encounter and finding proper solutions that will benefit the majority, with self-control and restraint in front of adults. There is also the teaching of patience and perseverance to strengthen their minds to be courageous in the wake of disaster."[425] When you instill in youth "it's OK to break things,"[426] along with the belief of a native people that never bragged or exaggerated things but just lived in accord with nature, any and all things become possible.

The instructor corps has been chosen to integrated with the introduction of Mr. Mark Elliot Zuckerberg,[427] along with Nogrod[428] of the Black Hills of South Dakota, and the Lakota Sioux,[429]. The Special Forces unit designation for this HBA is the United States Air Force Pararescuemen (PJ).[430] The process of becoming a PJ[431] is formally known as "Superman School." This special operations training course is almost two years long, making it one of the longest in the world. It also has one of the highest training attrition rates in the U.S. Special Operations community, at around 80%. Traditions are an important part of the education of our young boys as they become men. As we found among the Lakota Sioux,[432] there is also a creed amongst the PJ's[433] that authentically states:

CODE OF THE AIR RESCUE MAN

It is my duty, as a member of the Air Rescue Service, to save life and aid the injured.

I will be prepared at all times to perform my assigned duties quickly and efficiently, placing these duties before personal desires and comforts.

These things I do, THAT OTHERS MAY LIVE."[434]

NARGOTHROND[435]

Lawrence "Larry" Edward Page:[436]

CCT[437]—"MICHIGAN"—"OTTAWA AND CHIPPEWA"[438]—
"NARGOTHROND"[439]

Number nine (9) of the Honor Bound Academies[440] was inspired by
Menegroth[441] in Doriath, its name was Nargothrond.[442] Once again,
another creation from Tolkien's mind, a hidden place meant to be safe
from the forces of Morgoth.[443] *The Silmarillion*[444] continues to develop
a captivating mythology. "In this book, the story follows Finrod as he
establishes Nargothrond in the early years after the return of the Noldor
to Middle-Earth. The city is located in the caverns of Narog beneath
the forested hills of Taur-en-Foroth on the western bank of the Narog
River. Originally, a narrow path along the banks of the river was the
only way to reach it, but later, a bridge was built across the Narog. For
a location within the continental United States of this Honor Bound
Academy,[445] the Upper Peninsula of Michigan has been chosen. Additionally, our Patron Lawrence Edward Page, originally hails from Lan-
sing, Michigan."[446]

Mr. Lawrence Edward Page[447] as Patron is an American software
engineer and internet entrepreneur. He is best known as one of the
co-founders of Google. Mr. Page[448] is the co-inventor and namesake of
Pagebook, a search ranking algorithm for Google. During an interview,
Lawrence Edward Page[449] recalled his childhood noting that his house
"was usually a mess, with computers, science, and technology maga-
zines all over the place."[450] There was also a description of a father who
earned a PhD in computer science as the field was just being established,
and a mother who was an instructor in computer programming. "Page
was first attracted to computers when he was six years old, as he was
able to "play with the stuff lying around–first-generation personal computers—that had been left by his mother and father."[451]

Thanks to his older brother, who "taught him to take things apart,
and before long he was taking everything in his house apart to see how
it worked." He said "From a very early age, I also realized I wanted to

invent things. Probably from when I was 12, I knew I was going to start a company eventually."[452] From here, I believe it is appropriate to present the history of the last race of Native Americans now existing in the state of Michigan, called the Ottawa and Chippewa Nations of American natives.[453]

The Ottawa[454] were widely known as traders. Their location and negotiating skills enabled them to become middlemen in intertribal commerce. They were Algonquian-speaking North American Indians whose original territory centered on the Ottawa River, the French River, and Georgian Bay, in present-day Northern Michigan. Here, we exemplify, "the purpose and meaning of why to incorporate Native American tradition and heritage into the various Honor Bound Academies. [455] To better understand, I offer these words found in "The Lamentation of the Overflowing Heart of the Red Man of the Forest." [456]

"Hark! What is that I hear, So mournfully ringing in my ear, Like a death song of warriors, For those who fell by their brave sires? Is this the wail now sounding for my unhappy future?

O my destiny, my destiny! How sinks my heart, as I behold my inheritance all in ruins and desolation. Yes, desolation; the land the Great Spirit has given us in which to live, to roam, to hunt, and build our council fires, is no more to behold."[457]

To undo the harm inflicted upon these ancient people long ago, to restore their natural way of life, and to bring balance to the healing of old wounds. To regain strength by living in harmony with nature and revitalizing everything anew. The United States Air Force Combat Control Teams (CCT),[458] also known as "Combat Controllers,"[459] are responsible for these important tasks. As with all the various Honor Bound Academy[460] instructors, CCTs[461] bring about their own unique perspective. "The mission of a Combat Controller is to deploy undetected into combat and hostile environments to conduct special reconnaissance, establish assault zones or airfields, while simultaneously conducting air traffic control, fire support, command, control, communication and forward air control."[462] During an intensive, nearly two-yearlong initial training, with a "wash out rate upwards of 90–95%"[463] this training is one of the most rigorous in the U.S. military. To honor its patron Lawrence

Edward Page,[464] the state of Michigan, and the Ottawa,[465] along with their "Twenty-one Precepts or Moral Commandments of the Ottawa and Chippewa Indians,"[466] linked with the "CCT's motto: "First There," reaffirms the Combat Controller's commitment to undertaking the most dangerous missions behind enemy lines by leading the way for others forces to follow."[467]

GREY HAVENS[468]

Sergey Mikhailovich Brin:[469]

SR[470] — "MISSISSIPPI" — "NATCHEZ"[471] — "GREY HAVENS"[472]

We finally come to the last of the Honor Bound Academies,[473] created by a vision I've possessed for a very long time. I have titled or chosen as a header — "Adolescent Combat Diplomate,"[474] and utilized J. R. R. Tolkien's masterpiece *The Silmarillion.*[475] As with the prior academies, this will take the name of "Grey Havens."[476] The words I'll use to describe this are as such: "because of its cultural and spiritual importance to the elves, the Grey Havens in time became the primary Elven settlement west of the Misty Mountains prior to the establishment of Eregion, and later, Rivendell."[477] Even as the Elves dwindled in numbers by the year, the Grey Havens[478] remained a focal point of history in the northern part of Middle Earth. The location of the Grey Havens,[479] It will be along the Mississippi River in the Natchez Bluffs area of the Lower Mississippi Valley in the state of Mississippi.

The Patron for the Grey Havens[480] is Sergey Mikhailovich Brin,[481] who is also an American software engineer and internet entrepreneur. He was one of the individuals who, along with several of the Patrons, suspended their studies at Universities. In his case, it was Stanford, and he paused to create the start-up (Google) in a garage in Menlo Park. Sergey Mikhailovich Brin, along with HBA[482] Patron and Mr. Laurence Edward Page[483] (Nargothrond)[484] are both working on more personal projects that reach beyond Google. For instance, both are working to address the world's energy and climate challenges through Google's philanthropic arm, Google.org. They are investing in the alternative energy sector to discover more extensive sources of renewable energy. The company recognizes that its founders, like other Honor Bound Academy[485] Patrons, aim to tackle significant issues using technology. With the Grey Havens,[486] Mr. Sergey Brin,[487] its location in Mississippi and an opportunity to seek a bond with the Natchez[488] Native American people who originally populated this area. The Natchez[489] are noted for being the only Mississippi culture with complex Chiefdom characteristics to have survived long into the period after the European colonization of America began. The Natchez[490] are also noted for having had an "unusual social system of nobility classes and exogamous marriage practices. It was a strongly matrilineal kinship society, with descent reckoned along female lines. The paramount Chief, named Great Sun, was always the son of the female Sun, whose daughter would be the mother of the next Great Sun. This ensured that the Chiefdom stayed under the control of the single Sun lineage."[491]

During World War II, Army Air Force Combat Weathermen supported the American effort against the Japanese in the China-Burma-India theater of operations. They also participated in the European theater at Normandy Beach, France. "The SOWT (Special Operations Weather Team) battlefield airmen career field was recently renamed Special Reconnaissance on 30 April 2019, in order to bolster the Air Force Special Tactics teams—which consist of combat control, pararescue, and tactical air control party airmen—as they prepare for an era of great power competition."[492]

"SWOT's new role as Special Reconnaissance (SR), will shift a specialized weather analysis focus to one of multi-domain reconnaissance and surveillance."[493] "They operated on 2–3-man Environmental Reconnaissance Teams (ERT). ERTs were attached to 8–9-man Special Tactics Teams (STT) alongside Combat Control (CCT) and Pararescue (PJ) personnel. Together they provide SOCOM (Special Operations Command) a unique capability to establish and control austere airfields in permissive and non-permissive environments."[494] This expertise and knowledge, upon completion of their service to the country, will continue to present future generations of young American Honor Bound Academy[495] youth to the same level of professionalism.

In conclusion, this has been my introduction to the American public regarding my creation of Honor Bound Academies.[496] The focus of this program, presented in 10 different locations, is a "Rite of Passage."[497] Specifically, the academy is formed for youth eighteen, nineteen, and twenty years of age as they transition from adolescence to adulthood. More information can be found regarding my 501 (C) 3 non-profit Honor Bound Academy, Inc.[498] located at the web page located at *www. thehonorboundacademy.org.*

EPILOGUE

Here in closure, I wish to dispense three (3) final Cairns, left on the path of this journey.

One, I have acknowledged my participation with the Fraternal Order of UDT/SEAL's, along with the Organization of Freemasonry. It is my intention to bring honor, requesting your embrace as I walk through the Valley of the Shadow of Death.

Two, as an addict/alcoholic I see the destructive nature visited upon so many of my brothers and sisters. You must know by now there will be NO salvage from the hands of others. Through personal experience, I know as fact this journey must be sought within, and vital is it that purpose and meaning be found. I now stand before you, no different than you, bringing forth the purpose and meaning I found while looking within. There are so many worthy causes needing the attention of the stable hands created with all addicts and alcoholics in recovery. This I say to you, do not leave me alone, as I seek to address issues facing our youth. You are needed, along with your talents and abilities. Our time draws near.

Three, when first came the vision, it was seen not through the eyes of the masculine but clearly from the perspective of the feminine. All that you've read, is articulated from the male perspective. Yet, in my posses-sion is an entire dossier filled with knowledge labeled, Feminine Mys-tique. Just imagine Ms. Oprah Winfrey and Ms. Melinda Gates, what we, the three of us will do in bringing forth an Honor Bound Academy for our young women ages—18, 19, and 20, as they transition from adolescents to adulthood.

Here's to creating magic, as in years ago and days of old when truthfully it filled the air.

HONOR BOUND ACADEMY EXECUTIVE SUMMARY

SPRING 2024

A. PHILOSOPHY: Adolescence is a journey. It has always been the path from childhood to adulthood, and at a deeper level, the gateway to manhood and womanhood. Adolescence is a process of personal and developmental growth, and for tens of thousands of years adults have sculpted and created clear paths for adolescents to navigate. Modern culture has all but eliminated these time-tested approaches, leaving current teens to navigate the turbulent waters of adolescence without a map or guidance. Universally, almost every traditional culture came upon the same dynamics for helping their adolescents; mostly the deliveries differed. It's critical to remember that they did this for a reason: millennia of trial and error led almost all cultures, often isolated from other cultures and communities, to come to the same conclusion: that adolescents need to be guided forward in a clear and specific way to successfully reach adulthood.

Simply put, the adolescents in our society today need to be guided through the complex labyrinth of life. It is this confusing and difficult path to adulthood that Honor Bound Academy (HBA) seeks to lay straight for the majority of our society's male youth. Through a dynamic and challenging program of academic studies, meditation, travel, yoga, exercises to build es sprit de corps and Rites of Passage, these adolescents will develop the key to successfully navigating their chosen paths in life: a well-developed, powerful and pervasive sense of positive self-esteem.

B. PROBLEM STATEMENT: Statistics reveal that adolescent males in their late teenage years are increasingly becoming more in need of programs that will help to guide them through the confusing labyrinth of transitioning from childhood to adulthood. Crime, alcoholism and suicide rates continue to either increase or remain a significant problem in American society. We as a society are called to act.

C. SOLUTION CONCEPT/MISSION STATEMENT: Fifty selected males ages 18–20 years old will experience a fully-immersive, 365-day program called Honor Bound Academy (HBA) based in Sonoma County, CA, where a team consisting of a licensed clinical social worker, volunteer mentors, and staff will expose them to academic education, experiences, and counseling that will dramatically improve their self-esteem and instill in them a sense of honor. Honor Bound Academy will instill in them a philosophy that they are honor-bound: to themselves, their team-mates, and to society as a whole. Through this experience the program's goal is to help these teens develop their internal resources so as to realize their potential, converting potential burdens on society into productive, responsible contributors as mature and socially-responsible men.

D. HBA's FOUNDER/DIRECTOR: Honor Bound Academy is being founded by Mr. Thomas J. LaGrave, Jr. a licensed clinical social worker who served as a medical corpsman with the U.S. Navy SEAL's. He has over 30 years of experience working with youth.

E. HBA's STRATEGIC PARALLEL: Naval Basic Underwater Demoli-tion/Seal Training (Bud/S) Bud/S is the Naval Special Warfare Training Command that creates Naval Special Forces Operators (SEAL's). Each branch of the military has their own unique training commands. These training commands or schools utilize a very specific layered curriculum. The knowledge sources are intricately woven through the realms of the physical, intellectual, emotional and natural environments. The key to all military Special Forces training, and the underlying code of conduct essential to Navy SEAL's, is teamwork. It plays an incalculable role in movement, communication, successful mission objective and does so for a reason: "none of us is as good as all of us." Like BUD/S, HBA will focus on changing the student's mindset from "me" to "we."

F. HBA's MAXIM: Honor Bound Academy's maxim, or "general truth and principle" is "Vincit Qui Se Vincit—He Conquers Who Conquers Himself." It was carefully chosen for one simple reason: it drives home the principle that one must master his own self before one can master the world around him.

G. TARGET AUDIENCE: HBA is designed specifically for 18–20-year-old males who are especially in need of guidance. Not only teens with a history of drug/alcohol abuse, crime, or are disruptive products of the foster care system but all of America's youth are potential students for the program.

H. NUMBER OF STUDENTS: The first year of HBA's existence will be a 365-day pilot program consisting of fifty students. The intent is for these fifty original students to stay on as Student Mentors for a second year which will mirror the first year with regards to curriculum. Peer mentoring is a critical component of Honor Bound Academy. These original fifty students will serve to mentor the second year's incoming group of an additional fifty new students, bringing the total number of students for the second year of HBA's existence to 100.

I. LOCATION: Honor Bound Academy will be headquartered on a purchased/rented home on approximately 25–40 acres in Sonoma County, California. Dubbed, "The Ranch," this location was selected due to established relationships with local officials and its centralized location for activities such as scuba diving in Monterey Bay and nature-focused trips such as Yosemite National Park.

J. CURRICULUM: The 12-month program is broken down into three, 4-month phases, each with a corresponding focus and theme.

PHASE	TIME FRAME	FOCUS	THEME
1. Separation	months 1–4	Physical	"Fire"
2. Initiation	months 5–8	Nature	"Earth/Air'
3. Return	months 9–12	Self Awareness	"Water"

PHASE ONE

Separation (Educational Focus Areas of Symbols, Religions, & Empires)

Phase One begins with the fifty adolescents' arrival at Honor Bound Academy. Every stitch of clothing along with their shoes will be removed, washed, pressed and placed in storage. They will be given attire that is exactly alike for each student. The first month will be an introduction to the program. Various tests from educational competency, personality inventory, and occupational ability will be applied for a base line. At the end of Day One a communal meeting will be called to address one central question. The answer to this question begins the journey that is their "Rite of Passage" for this first phase. The question posed is, "Do you want to be here?"

The first three months will acclimate each youth to the structure of Honor Bound Academy. The weekday and weekend schedules will be posted at the beginning of each week, and strictly adhered to. The academic focus areas of Symbols, Myth, and Empires will culminate in the departure of staff and students for a month of travel to Jerusalem, Cairo, Rome, Stonehenge, and Washington D.C.

At this time the first of four Rites of Passage will be performed. It calls for a ceremonial gathering of all participants, their pressed attire which was stored upon arrival, and the use of **Fire**. Their Rite of Passage by Fire represents the purification/transition from their past by symbolically burning their old clothes accompanied by a declarative, personal statement of wanting to remain in the program.

PHASE TWO

Initiation (Educational Focus Areas of Environment, Human Development, Science & Art)

With the start of this phase, the popular physical fitness regimen of P–90–X will be introduced into the program. This is a three-month physical routine requiring a personal commitment and frequent self-assessment. The four-month interconnected educational components for this phase address Environment, Human Development, Science, and Art.

Honor Bound Academy's second Rite of Passage, the first for Phase Two, begins at the end of month two (week 24 of the overall program). This is the **Earth** Rite of Passage and all its elements; it will be a smaller version of the Navy SEAL's BUD/S program, serving to teach the students that they can move past the boundaries through which they think are present. It will last three days, incorporating physical, emotional, and intellectual challenges during a 72-hour period without sleep. (The exercise will be closely controlled for safety, with risk mitigation measures and full involvement of paramedics being present throughout the entire exercise.)

Constantly on the move, the only time they will rest is at meals. They will be cold, wet and miserable as they realize they possess a well of self-reliance, toughness, and resiliency that is stronger than what they ever though was possible. (West Coast Chapter UDT/SEAL (San Francisco) Association will participate in this exercise as mentors/moderators/safeties).

Phase Two's second Rite of Passage (third overall of the entire program) occurs during the final month of the Phase (week 32 of the overall program). The third Rite of Passage is that of **Air,** parachuting from the sky, as each student will execute a static line parachute jump through a commercial parachuting company. The confidence gained by successfully confronting this fear will serve to strengthen their self-esteem and confidence.

PHASE THREE

Return (Educational Focus Areas of Business, War, Self-Assessment, and Transition)

During the first week of Phase One the foundation for the fourth and final Rite of Passage was begun—**Water**. All of the young men were introduced to water; starting in a pool at the shallow end, they gradually progressed to swimming and teambuilding exercises in rivers and lakes. In the following months they made their way to the shallow bays of the Pacific Ocean and finally into the deeper parts, developing skills that will be critical during the final Rite of Passage. Body surfing, boogey boarding, and IBS (Inflatable Boat Small) surf passage are skills that will be developed, particularly IBS Surf Passage. This is an exercise that demands the highest level of teamwork.

At the onset of Phase Three, scuba diving will be taught for PADI certification. At the conclusion of Phase Three, the Rite of passage of **Water** will be performed. Two dives will take place in the ocean, one during the day and the second one at night in Monterey Bay. This will bring closure to the program's curriculum. (Safety is obviously the number one concern of the diving experience. The instructors will be Navy SEAL's who have earned their teaching certification through PADI (Professional Organization of Diving Instructors).

At the conclusion of the program, the students will participate in a solemn, night time culmination ceremony where each of them will receive a dagger and a ring. The dagger will be inscribed with the logo and motto of Honor Bound Academy, being a representative of a spear. In many ancient societies, a youth was presented a spear after completing their Rite of Passage, symbolizing that they as a warrior they had transitioned into being a man. The ring that each youth will receive symbolizes the eternal nature of the HBA experience—it will be designed by the group, serving as a connection to this experience where they passed into adulthood *having left childhood behind.* Through Honor Bound Academy, they will remember and cherish the memories and lessons of childhood and the Rites of Passage that led them through the labyrinth.

K. TRAVEL: One fourth of the way through the program (April), the students will experience the education and personal development that only travel in a foreign country can provide. This is far different than a "Spring Break" whirlwind tour: independent decision making/exploration in a controlled, safe environment will be stressed. Two students will be paired with one adult staff member as they experience the following locations for approximately five days each:

- Jerusalem, Israel
- Cairo, Egypt
- Rome, Italy
- Salisbury, England (Stonehenge)
- Washington D.C.

L. NATURE EXCURSIONS: Diverse and accessible, nature will serve as a powerful teaching tool as the students gain a better connection to the four areas that comprise the Rites of Passage: Fire, Earth, Air, and Water. The following locations are all within driving distance and several will be visited during both summer and winter settings):

- Yosemite National Park
- Lake Tahoe
- Lake Shasta

- Big Sur
- Armstrong Forest
- Mendocino County
- Pacific Coast Trail

M. YOGA & MEDITATION: The benefits of yoga and meditation with regards to the physical, emotional, and mental health of an individual are widely known and respected. As such, a certified yoga instructor will be part of Honor Bound Academy's staff, leading the students in both disciplines on an almost daily basis.

N. COST: The estimated cost to execute the program as outlined for the first two years is approximately $6,370,000. Cost-reduction measures such as renting the house/land vs. purchasing it could be considered. See the Business Plan (Annex B) of the Strategic Vision for the full outline of anticipated costs.

O. STAFF: In addition to a Board of Directors made up of volunteer consultants, the staff of Honor Bound Academy will consist of the following:

- Director/Founder/Primary Counselor: Mr. Thomas J. LaGrave, Jr.
- Eight Primary Staff Members (paid)
- Mentors (Volunteers—approximately 25): A duo of two student will be paired with a volunteer mentor.
- Yoga/Mediation Instructor (Paid): As previously discussed in this document.
- Cook/Housekeeper (Paid): This individual will prepare all meals and perform general housekeeping duties at The Ranch.

P. ADDITIONAL AREAS: Please see the full Strategic Vision for additional information regarding Measures of Effectiveness (MOEs), Schedules, Operational Requirements, Equipment Requirements, Academy Attire, Insurance, Phone/Internet policy and Family/Friend Visits policy. Additionally, the Strategic Vision includes the founder's full resume, Cost Analysis, and travel details.

"We have not even to risk the adventure alone; for the heroes of all time have gone before us; the labyrinth is thoroughly known; we have only to follow the thread of the hero-path, and where we had thought to find an abomination, we shall find a god. And where we had thought to slay another, we shall slay ourselves; . . . where we had thought to travel outward, we shall come to the center of our own existence. And where we had thought to be alone, we shall be with all the world."

—JOSEPH CAMPBELL, "The Hero's Adventure"

STRATEGIC VISION FOR HONOR BOUND ACADEMY

SPRING 2024

TABLE OF CONTENTS

Vehicles
Curriculum
Technology Employed
Staffing
Payroll
Financial Controls
Regulatory Compliance
Zoning
Certification
Licensing
Occupancy Permits
Management & Organization
Compensation
Financials

"Vincit Qui Se Vincit—He Conquers Who Conquers Himself"

I. INTRODUCTION

"We have not even to risk the adventure alone; for the heroes of all time have gone before us; the labyrinth is thoroughly known; we have only to follow the thread of the hero-path, and where we had thought to find an abomination, we shall find a god. And where we had thought to slay another, we shall slay ourselves; . . . where we had thought to travel out- ward, we shall come to the center of our own existence. And where we had thought to be alone, we shall be with all the world."

—JOSEPH CAMPBELL, "THE HERO'S ADVENTURE"

Adolescence is a journey. It has always been the path from child- hood to adulthood, and at a deeper level, the gateway to manhood and womanhood. Adolescence is a process of personal and developmental growth, and for tens of thousands of years adults have sculpted and cre- ated clear paths for adolescents to navigate.

Modern culture has all but eliminated these time-tested approaches, leaving current teens to navigate the turbulent waters of adolescence without a map or guidance. Universally, almost every traditional cul- ture came upon the same dynamics for helping their adolescents; mostly the deliveries differed. It's critical to remember that they did this for a reason: millennia of trial and error led almost all cultures, often isolated from other cultures and communities, to come to the same conclusion: that adolescents need to be guided forward in a clear and specific way to successfully reach adulthood.

Simply put, the adolescents in our society today need to be guided through the complex labyrinth of life. It is this confusing and difficult path to adulthood that Honor Bound Academy (HBA) seeks to lay straight for some of our society's most troubled male youths. Through a dynamic and challenging program of academic studies, meditation, travel, yoga, exercises to build es sprit de corps and Rites of Passage, these adolescents will develop the key to successfully navigating their chosen paths in life: a well-developed, powerful and pervasive sense of positive self-esteem.

II. PROBLEM STATEMENT

Statistics reveal that adolescent males in their late teenage years are increasingly becoming more in need of programs that will help to guide them through the confusing labyrinth of transitioning from childhood to adulthood. Crime, alcoholism and suicide rates continue to either increase or remain a significant problem in American society. Consider the recent results of major studies by the CDC (Center For Disease Control & Prevention):

- Alcohol use remains extremely widespread among our nation's teenagers. 39% of high school students reported that they had consumed alcohol, with 22% reporting that they had participated in binge drinking.

- Suicide is the third leading cause of death for death for youths ages 10–24. 16% of students reported seriously considering suicide, 13% reported creating a plan, and 8% reporting trying to take their own life. Boys are more likely than girls to die from suicide. Of the reported suicides in the 10 to 24 age group, 81% of the deaths were males and 19% were females.

- In 2010, 4,828 young people ages 10 to 24 were victims of homicide—an average of 13 each day. Homicide is the 2nd leading cause of death for young people ages 15 to 24 years old. Among homicide victims 10 to 24 years old in 2010, 86% (4,171) were male and 14% (657) were female.

- Nearly 33% of high school students reported being in a physical fight within the last 12 months and nearly 17 percent of males reported carrying a weapon to school (gun, knife, or club).

Teenagers already experiencing problems with the law and society as a whole are likely to continue down that path unless they are guided and developed into young adults capable of making positive choices.

III. SOLUTION CONCEPT/MISSION STATEMENT

Fifty selected males ages 18–20 years old will experience a fully-immersive, 365-day program called Honor Bound Academy based in Sonoma County, CA, where a team consisting of a licensed clinical social worker, volunteer mentors, and staff will expose them to education, experiences, and counseling that will dramatically improve their self-esteem and instill in them a sense of honor. *Honor Bound Academy will instill in them a philosophy that they are honor-bound: to themselves, their teammates, and to society as a whole.* Through this experience the program's goal is to help these teens develop their internal resources so as to realize their potential, converting potential burdens on society into productive, responsible contributors as mature and socially-responsible men.

IV. PHILOSOPHY OVERVIEW

The concept of honor is one long-held by upright, virtuous people. Honor is defined by the Webster Dictionary as," integrity in one's beliefs" and as such, Honor Bound Academy's philosophy is grounded in the military code of honor exhibited by members of the Navy SEAL's. Members of a SEAL team embrace the military code of honor, dedication, sacrifice for the greater good and a level of es sprit de corps rarely found in civilian life. Similar to the Navy's motto of, "Not For Self But Country," SEAL's live out a code of brotherhood in which they will give their life so that their brother may live. It is this sense of honor, of loyalty to oneself and the team, of a commitment to excellence, which Honor Bound Academy will instill in its students.

V. HBA'S FOUNDER/DIRECTOR

Honor Bound Academy is being founded by Mr. Thomas J. LaGrave, Jr. a licensed clinical social worker who served as a Hospital Corpsmen with the U.S. Navy SEAL's. Over a span of 30 years Tom La Grave has been focused on the physical and mental health of young adults and adolescents, along with their healing and personal development.

His early hospital and field duties as a Corpsman with the US Navy SEAL's, subsequent work with adolescent mental health and chemical dependency programs, the management of the psychiatric and social problems of young prison inmates, and finally, his position as a Military Family & Life Consultant for the US Armed Forces Special Operations Command, have all sharply honed his insight into the adolescent world and the psychological and developmental challenges facing youth transitioning to manhood in today's society. His involvement with a variety of programs responding to the psychological and behavioral disorders, and the physical problems, as well as the social and personal identity deficits and dysfunctions characteristic of this age/gender group, has led to a clear understanding of what works and what doesn't work. He is committed to constructing and implementing a program that can provide individual tools for the majority of youth to deal with their personal and social development challenges in 21st century America. (please see Appendix A for Mr. LaGrave's resume).

VI. WHAT HBA STANDS FOR

A. Principles

Adolescence can be viewed in the mythological way of the labyrinth. Most people do not realize there is a distinct difference between a labyrinth and a maze. A maze is built to be confusing to the participant. Blind alleys and blocked paths confuse and confound the traveler, making this journey difficult and frustrating. Conversely, a labyrinth is a single guided path, allowing a clear direction to the center and back out again. Without the confusion and frustration of a maze, labyrinths offer a more subtle, internally-focused trip where one learns from the quietness within.

Modern culture has created a scenario where adolescents are expected to get through the maze on their own. The maze is what happens when we look at adolescence as "a phase to get through." The maze creates anger and much failure along the way, often leading the traveler nowhere at all. Getting stuck is common, which often leads to frustration and quitting.

The universal structure of initiations and rites of passage were built on the principle of the labyrinth: to create a clear and simple path to adulthood without all the negativity, difficulty, and arbitrariness of the maze. *This simple path was created, supported and mentored by those who had walked it previously.* The labyrinth represents a trail followed by countless others before, marked clearly for future generations to follow. Like the rock cairns left on a meandering trail by the person who walked there prior, these trails were monitored and maintained for all to use. Many or most of the 'guides' were the elders, giving back and passing on their knowledge. Sadly, elder mentors have become almost extinct in this day of forced retirement, moving to warmer climates, or broken homes being common.

Thus, today's teens meander an unmarked trail, the rock cairn aids discarded and ignored. They plow ever forward, stumbling into the blocked passages and closed pathways, looking for signs or clues to the correct direction but not finding them. There are no clear criteria for them to follow or emulate, and they often become lost or take the wrong path.

We, the former travelers of adolescence, are required by love, history, and experience to create clearer paths for our youth, to provide maps for them to follow, and to remodel our society's maze into a labyrinth. One of the great crimes in modern times has been to steal these cairns from our youth as they try to find their way on their own... and our second greatest crime as a society has been in holding this irresponsibility and lack of guidance against them.

Basic Underwater Demolition/ SEAL (BUD/S) Training has been the Director's personal labyrinth or "Rite of Passage." Today, the civilian realm of adolescence is at a crossroad; a need has emerged. In our modern society the rites for marking the divisions between the stages of life are mechanical, ill-defined, or nonexistent. It is out of the fires of society's great need that Honor Bound Academy is being forged.

B. HBA's Strategic Parallel: Naval Basic Underwater Demolition/Seal Training (BUD/S)

BUD/S is the Naval Special Warfare Training Command that creates Naval Special Forces Operators (SEAL's). Each branch of the military has their own unique training commands. These training commands or schools utilize a very specific layered curriculum. The knowledge sources are intricately woven through the realms of the physical, intellectual, emotional and natural environments. Not only is it part classroom, part real-world, but through the merger of these two domains an underlying code of conduct emerges. Honor Bound Academy's philosophy has a strong strategic parallel to the BUD/S program.

The key to all military Special Forces training, and the underlying code of conduct essential to Navy SEAL's, is teamwork. This critical component is the cornerstone of a transition from "me" to "we." It plays an incalculable role in movement, communication, successful mission objective and does so for a reason: "none of us is as good as *all* of us."

BUD/S has three phases, each lasting two months. The first phase is physical conditioning which includes basic classroom education. The second phase is Dive Phase, beginning in the pool and finishing in the ocean. It too has a classroom component (diving physics, underwater cartography, combat diving). The third phase is land warfare, taking in all the natural settings (desert, mountains, jungle, swamp, etc.). The classroom and outdoor activities address land navigation, small-unit tactics, patrolling techniques, rappelling, infantry tactics, and military explosives. Training is incremental and spans a six-month period establishing a thought process, a framework. Though each of the three phases is separate, they're in actuality intimately connected.

Due to this intimate connection, an awareness within each individual begins to take shape. BUD/S training and its curriculum mirror this statement as it creates a very unique and specific mind set. It fosters the individual in conjunction with others to overcome insurmountable obstacles, to believe that anything is possible. How is this done? *It is done by using the natural environment.* Honor Bound Academy's mindset and organization will be similar to the BUD/S program in that it will be established in a rural setting (external nature), the Director and staff are all Navy SEAL's (internal nature). With this combination both the school and staff create a powerful emergence or awareness in the youth, (conscious/unconscious).

The differential aspect of Honor Bound Academy from BUD/S is found in the spiritual. This is crucial: *the key aspect that separates the two programs is the integration of meditation.* The altering of the curriculum in this way will not diminish; rather it will enhance the overall goal. For self-actualization an individual must search within.

C. HBA's Emblem:

As previously described, the labyrinth signifies a clear and simple path to adulthood. Far different than the confusion, negativity, and bewilderment of a maze, it is an identifiable trail marked by others in the youth's journey to maturity. HBA's colors of gray and green have symbolic meaning: the gray symbolizes that there are few black and white answers in life and the color of green symbolizes all the elements that characterize the program's curriculum: Fire, Earth, Air, and Water.

D. HBA's Maxim:

Honor Bound Academy's maxim, or "general truth and principle" is "*Vincit Qui Se Vincit—He Conquers Who Conquers Himself.*" It was carefully chosen for one simple reason: it drives home the principle that one must master his own self before he can master the world around him. Knowledge of thyself. Self-Control. Self-Discipline. Though they oftentimes may feel that the world around them is spinning out of control and is in chaos, they will learn that they **can** control their reaction to it and determine their own destiny. In the words of the English poet William Ernest Henley in the poem "Inviticus,"

> It matters not how strait the gate,
> How charged with punishments the scroll.
> I am the master of my fate
> I am the captain of my soul

The Latin translation of this phrase symbolizes the educational emphasis of Honor Bound Academy. As outlined in the curriculum portion of this proposal, the program stresses an intense study of language, governments, and societies: it is therefore quite appropriate that Latin, as the foundation for all language, be a key component of Honor Bound Academy's maxim.

VII. PROGRAM DESCRIPTION

A. Mission Statement

Fifty selected males ages 18–20 years old will experience a fully-immersive, 365-day program called Honor Bound Academy based in Sonoma County, CA, where a team consisting of a licensed clinical social worker, volunteer mentors, and staff will expose them to education, experiences, and counseling that will dramatically improve their self-esteem and instill in them a sense of honor. *Honor Bound Academy will instill in them a philosophy that they are honor-bound: to themselves, their teammates, and to society as a whole.* Through this experience the program's goal is to help these teens develop their internal resources so as to realize their potential, converting potential burdens on society into productive, responsible contributors as mature and socially-responsible men.

B. Target Audience

HBA is designed specifically for 18–20-year-old males who are especially in need of guidance. Not just for teens with a history of drug/alcohol abuse, crime, or are disruptive products of the foster care system but all youth of this age are potential students for the program, as the Director (Mr. Thomas J. LaGrave, Jr.) has extensive experience and certification in those areas. Please see the portion "Selecting Clients" in Appendix B for a detailed description of the selection process.

C. Number of Students

The first year of HBA's existence will be a 365-day pilot program consisting of fifty students. The intent is for these fifty original students to stay on as Student Mentors for a second year which will mirror the first year with regards to curriculum. Peer mentoring is a critical component of Honor Bound Academy. These original fifty students will serve to mentor the second year's incoming group of fifty new students, bringing the total number of students for the second year of HBA's existence to 100.

D. Location

Honor Bound Academy will be headquartered on a purchased/rented home on approximately 25–40 acres in Sonoma County, California. Dubbed, "The Ranch," this location was selected due to established relationships with local officials and its centralized location for activities such as scuba diving in Monterey Bay and nature-focused trips such as Yosemite National Park. Please see "Facilities" in appendix B for a detailed description of equipment, furnishings, vehicles, etc.

E. Program Pillars

Instilling a sense of honor is the overarching goal of the program. To support that goal there are six fundamentals, or "pillars," to the Honor Bound Academy program. The first five are the steps Andrew Newberg identified in his book, with applicable definitions created by HBA's founder. The sixth pillar is being added by the program's founder, as it is interwoven throughout nearly everything a student will experience:

> **Desire**—Students must WANT to be part of the program, as it is voluntary. Students are free to leave the program at any time.
>
> **Focus**—Students will develop/sharpen their abilities to focus through dedicated study of government, history, religion, science, business and art.
>
> **Mind/Body/Emotion Control**—Developing one's ability to find inner peace and concentration during chaos will be accomplished through yoga and meditation.
>
> **Practice**—Students will put their newly-developed skills and independence into practice through exercises in skydiving, open-water diving, and travel to foreign countries.

Expectation—Much like faith with regards to belief, the students will develop a self-expectation that they can and will accomplish their goals.

Counseling—Regular counseling sessions with the licensed Director, both on an individual and group basis, will be a critical component of the program where it will be interwoven with the other 5 pillars.

VIII. CURRICULUM

Overview

Countless generations from many tribes and societies guided their youth through initiation practices, enduring and surviving rites of passage. Mythology expert Joseph Campbell synthesized this process for us in his Hero's Journey. He broke down this elaborate system into three phases: Separation, Initiation, and Return. While Initiation, Rites of Passage, and the Hero's Journey seem to be synonymous, and they are certainly interrelated, they each have a distinct flavor to them.

The 12-month program is broken down into three, 4-month phases, each with a corresponding focus and theme. Detailed curriculum details will be outlined in the sections following this overview:

PHASE	TIME FRAME	FOCUS	THEME
1. Separation	months 1–4	Physical	"Fire"
2. Initiation	months 5–8	Nature	"Earth/Air"
3. Return	months 9–12	Self Awareness	"Water"

PHASE ONE — SEPARATION (EDUCATIONAL FOCUS AREAS OF SYMBOLS, RELIGIONS, & EMPIRES)

On the path to adulthood, Initiation is the *process* of the trip, the need to move up and forward. It is the understanding that growth is up there, further ahead on the path. If an initiate's challenge is to cross a great river, that would be his or her Rite of Passage, the challenge they would need to overcome. *Challenge is the key ingredient in rites of passage, and risk is the key to growth.*

Phase One begins with the fifty adolescents' arrival at Honor Bound Academy. Every stitch of clothing along with their shoes will be removed, washed, pressed and placed in storage. They will be given attire that is exactly alike for each student. The first month will be an introduction to the program. Various tests from educational competency, personality inventory, and occupational ability will be applied for a base line. At the end of Day One a communal meeting will be called to address one central question. The answer to this question begins the journey that is their "Rite of Passage" for the this first phase. The question posed is, "Do you want to be here?" Do you accept the call to this adventure?" If the answer is "YES," then state your full name and say the words "I—John Smith—accept the challenge of this adventure."

The first three months will acclimate each youth to the structure of Honor Bound Academy. The weekday and weekend schedules will be posted at the beginning of each week, and strictly adhered to. The educational focus areas of Symbols, Myth, and Empires will culminate in the departure of staff and students from Continental United States (CONUS) for a month of travel to Jerusalem, Cairo, Rome, Stonehenge, and Washington D.C. (see section 8C for a full description). Upon completion of the fourth month the students/staff will arrive back in CONUS at Honor Bound Academy.

At this time the first of four Rites of Passage will be performed. It calls for a ceremonial gathering of all participants, their pressed attire which was stored upon arrival, and the use of Fire. Their Initiation by Fire represents the purification/transition from their past by symbolically burning their old clothes accompanied by a declarative, personal statement. The ceremony will close with each being asked, "Do you want to be here?" Do you accept the call to continue this adventure? If the answer is "YES," then state your full name and say the words "I—John Smith—continue to accept the challenge of this adventure."

PHASE TWO — INITIATION (EDUCATIONAL FOCUS AREAS OF ENVIRONMENT, HUMAN DEVELOPMENT, SCIENCE & ART)

The Initiation By Fire that concluded Phase One separated the adolescents from their past. With Phase Two it is critical to intensify and build upon all the experiences from Phase One. With the start of this phase, the popular physical fitness regimen of P–90–X will be introduced into the equation. This is a three-month physical routine requiring a personal commitment and frequent self-assessment. The four-month interconnected educational components for this phase address Environment, Human Development, Science, and Art. Cumulatively they strengthen the view that each youth is part of something larger than themselves and connect them with the historical aspect of civilization development.

Honor Bound Academy's second Rite of Passage, the first for Phase Two, begins at the end of month two (week 24 of the overall program). This is the **Earth** Rite of Passage and all its elements; it will be a shorter version of the Navy SEAL's "Hell Week," serving to teach the students that they can move past the bounds through which they think are present. It will last three days, incorporating physical, emotional, and intellectual challenges during a 72-hour period without sleep. The exercise will be closely controlled for safety, with risk mitigation measures and full involvement of paramedics being present throughout the entire exercise. Constantly on the move, the only time they will rest is at meals. They will be cold, wet and miserable as they realize they possess a well of self-reliance, toughness, and resiliency that is stronger than what they ever thought was possible. (West Coast Chapter UDT/SEAL (San Francisco) Association will participate in this exercise as mentors/moderators/safeties).

Phase Two's second Rite of Passage (third overall of the entire program) occurs during the final month of the Phase (week 32 of the overall program). By now the students have completed two Rites of Passage and the routine P–90–X. They have faced fear in regards to physical stamina, the elements, and personal demons. Now another fear is confronted through the Rite of Passage by **Air.** This will require the same intestinal fortitude, facing of primal fear, and doing so from a unique perspective.

The third and final Rite of Passage of phase two is parachuting from the sky, as each student will execute a static line parachute jump through a commercial parachuting company. The confidence gained by successfully confronting this fear will serve to strengthen their self-esteem and confidence.

PHASE THREE—RETURN (EDUCATIONAL FOCUS AREAS OF BUSINESS, WAR, SELF-ASSESSMENT, AND TRANSITION)

The Rite of Passage of Air brought the second phase of the program to a close. In the beginning of Phase Three the young men will be asked to answer the initial question for a third time. "Do you want to be here?" Do you accept the call to continue this adventure? If the answer is "YES," then state your full name and say the words "I—John Smith—accept the challenge of this adventure." During third phase the educational components embrace Business, War, Self-Assessment, and Transition. Whereas the academic areas are again intensified, the physical challenges will be focused through a different environment.

During the first week of Phase One the foundation for the fourth and final Rite of Passage was begun—**Water**. All of the young men were introduced to water; starting in a pool at the shallow end, they gradually progressed to swimming and teambuilding exercises in rivers and lakes. In the following months they made their way to the shallow bays of the Pacific Ocean and finally into the deeper parts, developing skills that will be critical during the final Rite of Passage. Body surfing, bogey boarding, and IBS (Inflatable Boat Small) surf passage are skills that will be developed, particularly IBS Surf Passage. With loyalty being a cornerstone of Honor Bound Academy, this skill will be emphasized as it requires a very high level of teamwork.

At the onset of Phase Three, scuba diving will be taught for PADI certification. The physical endeavors of this phase will focus on water competency. At the conclusion of Phase Three, the Rite of passage of Water will be performed. Two dives will take place in the ocean, one during the day and the second one at night in Monterey Bay. This will bring closure to the program's curriculum. (Safety is obviously the number one concern of the diving experience. The instructors will be

Navy SEAL's who have earned their teaching certification through PADI (Professional Organization of Diving Instructors). All dive training will be in accordance with the strict curriculum of PADI Dive Certification).

DAGGER & RING

At the conclusion of the program, the students will participate in a solemn, night time culmination ceremony where each of them will receive a dagger and a ring. The dagger will be inscribed with the logo and motto of Honor Bound Academy, being a representative of a spear. In many ancient societies, a youth was presented a spear after completing their Rite of Passage, symbolizing that they as a warrior had transitioned into being a man. The ring that each youth will receive symbolizes the eternal nature of the HBA experience—it will be designed by the group, serving as a connection to this experience where they passed into adulthood *having left childhood.* Through Honor Bound Academy, they will remember and cherish the memories and lessons of childhood and the Rites of Passage that led them through the labyrinth.

At the onset of Honor Bound Academy FIRE separated each youth from their symbolic past. Through the Rites Passage of AIR and EARTH, the youth learned to reach deep within themselves to go beyond their personal belief system and self-conceived limits. Through the final Rite of Initiation by WATER they entered into a foreign world by leaving the surface and descending. Upon ascending from the depths they returned, cleansed and forever changed by the experience. Along each step of their journey they were guided by mentors offering them the wisdom of aged men, building cairns along the path to help the adolescent to navigate their own personal labyrinth. Through the year-long process of education, travel, meditation, yoga, and their four Rites of Passages, their transition from child to adulthood is nearly complete. As they leave Honor Bound Academy, they do so wrapped in the attire of manhood, prepared for life's many challenging journeys.

B. Classroom Academics

A critical component on HBA is the academic focus areas. Through these areas of study the young men will gain an understanding and appreciation for the ancient and modern cornerstones of mankind's being, simultaneously providing them a sense for the past and stretching their minds when considering what they may decide is in their future. Approximately two hours per weekday will be devoted to academics with corresponding study time. While academics are indeed fundamental in the program, the relatively low number of hours spent on "school" topics is intentional. The educational aspect of HBA goes far beyond the classroom: meditation, yoga, travel, and one-on-one counseling will have an equal or greater importance than what is discussed in an academic environment. These subjects will be taught by volunteer subject matter experts (for example, one of the program's volunteer mentors has earned a Master's of Business Administration—he will teach the classes centered on Business).

The following is an outline of academics that will be taught:

JANUARY (SYMBOLS)

1. History of Flags
2. Create Personal Flags
3. History of Heraldry: Family Crest
4. Create Family Crest

FEBRUARY (RELIGION)

*Note: Education on the basic fundamentals and history of these religions will be the focus. The leadership/instructors/mentors will not seek to influence the students in any way with regards to their religious practice or spiritual choice.

1. Pagan
2. Judaism
3. Christianity
4. Islam

MARCH (EMPIRES)

1. Persian
2. Egyptian
3. Roman
4. American

APRIL

*Spent traveling as described in section C

*Concludes with First Fire Rite of Passage: "Fire"

MAY (ENVIRONMENT)

1. Nature
2. Oceans
3. Air / Land
4. Space / Universe

JUNE (HUMAN DEVELOPMENT)

1. Evolution
2. Anthropology
3. Sociology
4. Spirituality

*Begins with Second Rite of Passage: "Earth"

JULY (SCIENCE)

1. Newtonian Physics (Classical Mechanics)
2. Analytical Psychology
3. Neurology
4. Quantum Physics (Quantum Mechanics)

AUGUST (ART)

1. The Classical Ideal—Romanesque and Gothic
2. The Early Renaissance—The High Renaissance
3. The Baroque—Age of Reason
4. Impressionism—Modern

*Concludes with Third Rite of Passage: "Air"

SEPTEMBER (BUSINESS/LEADERS)

1. Social Leaders
2. Titans of Industry
3. Generals/Admirals
4. Political Leaders

OCTOBER (WAR)

1. Sword (Ancient)
2. Gun Powder (Pre-Industrial)
3. Bombs (Industrial)
4. Nuclear (Modern)

NOVEMBER (MYTH)

1. Joseph Campbell—The Power of Myth
2. Native American Indians—The Power of Tribes
3. Greek Mythology
4. Roman Mythology

*Self-Assessment Exercises conducted throughout the month)

DECEMBER (TRANSITION)

1. Separation
2. Initiation
3. Return

* Fourth Rite of Passage: "Water"
* Concluding Ceremony

C. Travel

1. IMPORTANCE

One fourth of the way through the program (April), the students will experience the education and personal development that only travel in a foreign country can provide. By experiencing the customs, history, and culture of five different countries, the youths will improve their self-esteem and confidence by discovering that they can meet the challenges when thrust outside the comforts of their American way of life. They will gain a better appreciation for what they have, their eyes and minds will be greatly opened to the fact that there is so much more to the world than just what they have known thus far in their young lives. This is far different than a "Spring Break" whirlwind tour: independent decision making/exploration in a controlled, safe environment will be stressed. Local guides at each location, experts on the culture and history of their area, will assist in the planning and execution of the travel experiences.

2. LOCATIONS

Two students will be paired with one adult Staff Mentor as they experience the following locations for approximately five days each:

- Jerusalem, Israel
- Cairo, Egypt
- Rome, Italy
- Salisbury, England (Stonehenge)
- Washington D.C.

JERUSALEM—Jerusalem is the origin of one of the world's major religions and is one of the most historic cities in the world. The students will gain a better understanding of the importance that spiritual faith plays in the human race by literally standing on one of the major bedrocks of religion.

CAIRO—The students' exposure to the Egyptian Pyramids will bring about the realization that some things that mankind is capable of are enduring and have stood the test of time. As they touch the last of the original Wonders of the World, they will realize that the technology, fads, and cultural icons of today will fade away...and that what they leave behind, what they choose as their legacy can remain for generations.

ROME—As one of civilization's great pillars of society, the youths will have instilled in them a greater understanding of government, religion and culture. Through such experiences as being in The Pantheon, Vatican, and The Coliseum they will go through a life-shaping experience that cannot be found in books.

STONEHENGE—In the opinion of many, our current generation has a lack of understanding of just how precious life is, having a tendency to see their world as very small and revolving around themselves. At Stonehenge, visited both during the day and night, they will "look up at the stars through man's ancient understanding of celestial alignment. They will learn to push beyond what they think is out there beyond themselves while simultaneously looking deep within themselves.

WASHINGTON D.C.—One of the important academic areas of study is that of government. By the time the young men visit Washington D.C., they will have been exposed to the birthplaces of some of the most influential governmental systems in the history of time. Now in Washington D.C., they will gain a better understanding and appreciation for democracy. George Washington made our democracy. Abraham Lincoln stood in the breech to preserve it. Now as the students visit the Mall, standing between the Washington and Lincoln Memorials, they will understand the honor, courage, and beliefs that it took for them to define what greatness is in a man. A visit to Arlington Cemetery, experiencing the Changing of the Guard, will help them to understand the enormous sacrifices made for this democracy and our very way of life.

D. Nature Excursions

1. IMPORTANCE

California is home to some of the most stunning and beautiful natural environment on earth. Diverse and accessible, nature will serve as a powerful teaching tool as the students gain a better connection to the four areas that comprise the Rites of Passage: Fire, Earth, Air, and Water. Here the students will not only be exposed to and gain an appreciation for our environment on earth, the serene and powerful scenery will serve as a valuable setting in practicing meditation and yoga.

2. LOCATIONS

All of the destinations are within driving distance of the HBA Ranch. A total of 10 excursions will be conducted over the course of the year-long program:

- Yosemite National Park (Both Summer & Winter)
- Lake Tahoe (Both Summer & Winter)
- Lake Shasta
- Big Sur
- Armstrong Forest
- Mendocino County
- Pacific Coast Trail (both Summer & Winter)

E. Yoga & Meditation

Dr. Andrew Newberg is the Director of Research at the Myrna Brind Center for Integrative Medicine at Thomas Jefferson University Hospital and Medical College. His respected opinion on meditation is that, "in meditation, as in therapy, we learn to watch our negativity and not react to it. In the process, we train the brain to remain calm, even in the face of adversity. Thus, meditation becomes an exemplary way to reevaluate life's difficulties and mysteries. But perhaps most important, it trains the mind to become less attached to its own desires, attachments, and beliefs. When this happens, the way we see ourselves and the world will change." He goes on to say, "By manipulating our breath, body, awareness, feelings, and thoughts, we can decrease tension and stress. We can evoke or suppress specific emotions and focus our thoughts in ways that biologically influence other parts of the brain. From a neuroscientific perspective, this is astonishing because it upsets the traditional view that we cannot voluntarily influence nonconscious areas in the brain."

Through all the years of his extensive experience in working with troubled youth, the Director's conclusion is that most youth believe they are invincible, capable of overcoming any adversity. They sense various aspects of themselves, yet are unaware of the exact nature of their inner being. It is this very thing, this intangible, their inner being, that Honor Bound Academy seeks to awaken within. Meditation is a key component in reaching this goal. The practice of yoga will go hand-in-hand with meditation. The benefits of yoga with regards to physical, emotional, and mental realms of an individual are widely known and respected. As such, a certified yoga instructor will be part of Honor Bound Academy's staff, leading the students in both disciplines on an almost daily basis.

F. Typical Schedule

Below are samples of both a typical and weekday scheduled, modified appropriately as needed to incorporate travel, weather, Rites of Passage, and what the staff determines is most beneficial for the students.

* The hours of waking and bedtime are in accordance with teenage Circadian Rhythms.

WEEKDAY

11 a.m.—12 p.m.—Wake up, personal hygiene, snack*

12–1 p.m.—Yoga/Meditation

1–2 p.m.—Lunch

2–4 p.m.—Classroom Education

4–5 p.m.—Exercise, weight, cardio-vascular

5–6 p.m.—Dinner

6–8 p.m.—Outdoor Education

8–10 p.m.—Study Time

10–11 p.m.—Group Session (Overview of day's activities)

11–11:30 p.m.—One-to-One Counseling (Clinical): Each student receives minimum of once per week

11:30 p.m.–12 a.m.—Meditation

12–1 a.m.—Personal Time

1–2 a.m.—Stand Down/Quiet Time

2 a.m.—Lights out*

SATURDAY

11 a.m.–12 p.m.—Wake up, personal hygiene, snack*

12--1 p.m.—Yoga/Meditation

1–2 p.m.—Lunch

2–6 p.m.—Nature Trip

7–8 p.m.—Dinner

8–11 p.m.—Study Time

11–11:30 p.m.—Meditation

11:30–2 a.m.—Personal Time

2 a.m.—Lights out*

SUNDAY

(Note: students will be afforded to attend worship services of their choice in the surrounding area with transportation being provided)

11 a.m. –12 p.m.—Wake up, personal hygiene, snack*

12–1 p.m.—Yoga/Meditation

1–2 p.m.—Lunch

2–4 p.m.—Study Time

4–6 p.m.—Personal Time

6–7 p.m.—Dinner

7–8 p.m.—Personal Time

8–9 p.m.—Group Session (Past Week's Activities)

9–11 p.m.—Personal Time

11–11:30 p.m.—Meditation

11:30–2 a.m.—Personal Time

2 a.m.—Lights out*

IX. APPLIED TESTING

Each student's progress will be aided through the application of several tests, designed to provide both feedback and act as a guide for their strengths during the labyrinth ahead. These tests will be applied throughout the program:

- Personality Tests
- Achievement Tests
- Aptitude Tests
- Occupational Tests

X. COST

The estimated cost to execute the program as outlined in this Strategic Vision for the first two years is approximately $6,370,000. Cost-reduction measures such as renting the house/land vs. purchasing it could be considered. See appendix B for the full outline of anticipated costs.

XI. FACILITIES

("The Ranch—aka "Khazad Dum") Purchased/Rented home (with sufficient housing for 100+ youth) plus guesthouse (classroom) on 25–40 acres (required for outdoor education).

XII. LOGISTICAL/EQUIPMENT NEEDS

Initial outfitting of The Ranch will require the following:

- Classroom: Desks, chairs, computers with internet, printers, office supplies, etc.
- Household Good/Kitchen Furnishings
- Linen, bedroom furniture for students
- Three 10-passenger vans, 2–40 seat Buses

A set of equipment for the initial fifty students plus cadre would be needed at the program's onset. Additional equipment would be needed for the second year, as first year graduates of the program would remain as mentors.

A. BACKCOUNTRY

1. Cold weather clothing (layered, one set per student)
2. Cold weather sleeping bags
3. Tents
4. Cross-Country packs to include hydration systems/water purifiers
5. Stoves/Cooking Utensils
6. Rappelling Equipment (Ropes, Carbineers, etc.)

B. WATER

1. Wetsuits
2. Life jackets
3. Booties
4. Fins
5. Boogie Boards
6. Inflatable boats (two)
7. Paddles
8. PADI Certification Costs
9. Open water ocean dive costs (rental air tanks, powered boat, etc.)

C. AIR

1. Classroom academics plus one static line jump (commercial skydiving company)

D. VIDEO/LANGUAGE LIBRARIES

Videos from the following documentary series will be an integral part of classroom academics:

1. History Channel

2. Discovery Channel

3. National Geographic

4. Art & Entertainment Channel

5. Science Channel

6. Rosetta Stone Language Instruction

XIII. STUDENT'S PERSONAL GEAR REQUIREMENTS (BROUGHT WITH THEM)

A. Documents: Driver's License, Passport

B. Medications as needed (supervised by a licensed doctor)

C. ATM/Credit Card

D. Two pairs pants (jeans and slacks)

E. Eight pairs socks/underwear

F. Two pairs of shoes (athletic and dress)

G. T-shirts/sweatpants

F. One collared shirt

G. Two coats (casual and sport)

XIV. ACADEMY ATTIRE (PROVIDED)

Colors will be green and gray (HBA colors)

A. Reversible Green/Gray Sweatshirts—three

B. Shorts—three sets

C. Sweatpants—three sets

D. Wool socks—seven pairs

E. Swim trunks—three sets

F. Jungle Boots—two sets

G. Raincoat—one

XV. INSURANCE

Honor Bound Academy will carry the appropriate amount of protection/liability insurance for the location, equipment, and coverage of its staff. Students must have their own provided medical coverage.

XVI. CELL PHONE/INTERNET

All students would have full internet access, as well as cell phones provided by HBA.

XVII. FAMILY/FRIENDS ACCESS

Students would have the opportunity (but not required) to visit with their family and friends on Sundays as the schedule allows. Other arrangements can be made as needed.

XVIII. MEASURES OF EFFECTIVENESS (MOES)

HBA places a premium on making measurable changes in the clients and will utilize a series of scholarly and well recognized Measures of Effectiveness (MOEs). Ultimately, these MOE's will allow for determination of effectiveness of HBA upon the client.

DIRECTOR'S QUALIFICATIONS

Thomas J. La Grave, Jr.
M.S.W., L.C.S.W., BCD, CWT, DAAETS

LICENSED
Board of Behavioral Sciences, California

BOARD CERTIFIED
American Academy of Experts in Traumatic Stress American Board of Examiners in Social Welfare

CITIZENSHIP
United States of America

EDUCATION
1977–1978 St Mary's College, Moraga, CA

1990–1996 Skyline College, San Bruno, CA

B.S. 1998–2000 Cornerstone University, Grand Rapids, MI

M.S.W. 2000–2002 University of California Los Angeles, Los Angeles, CA

LICENSURE
- Board Certified Diplomate | License BCD #57262
- Licensed Clinical Social Worker | License CSW #23800
- Certified War Trauma | License CWT #6188
- Board Certified Diplomate | License DAAETS #6188

MILITARY SERVICE

United States Navy (1979–1988)

Naval Special Warfare (UDT/SEAL)Hospital Corpsmen

Three Commands: UDT-22, SEAL Team 2, and SEAL Team 1

Basic Underwater Demolition/SEAL Training

(BUD/S Class #106)

Duties included: platoon corpsmen, leading petty officer in medical department, proficiency in the application of field medicine, provided primary unsupervised medical support as deployed corpsmen.

Basic Hospital Corp "A" School

Emergency Medical Technician

ASSOCIATIONS & MEMBERSHIPS

- Alumni Association—UCLA
- Alumni Association—Cornerstone University
- Society for Social Work and Research
- International Brotherhood of Teamsters Local #85
- Freemasonry, Temple Lodge #14
- Fraternal Order of UDT/SEAL Association
- UDT/SEAL Museum Association
- Veterans of Foreign Wars (VFW)
- American Board of Examiners for Clinical Social Work
- EMDR International Association July 2016—Present
- Joseph Campbell Foundation, Mar 2016—Present
- C. G. Jung Institute of San Francisco, Jan 2015—Present
- National Center for Crisis Management (NCCM) Membership #6188

- American Academy of Experts in Traumatic Stress (AAETS)
- Diplomate/Certified War Trauma Membership #20122
- Special Operations Medical Association (SOMA) Membership #00975390
- American Psychological Association (APA) Membership #205635771
- Department of California the American Legion

AWARDS & HONORS

University of California Los Angeles (CalSWEC Title 4-E) $37,000 stipend

Cornerstone University, Distinguished Achievement Award

United States Navy Honorable Discharge

PUBLICATIONS

Honor Bound Academy

The Bell Tolls for Thee: A Soliloquy, Amazon Books, 2018.

At this time, I am collaborating with Special Operations Medical Association (SOMA) and the American Psychological Association (APA) in order to submit a number of articles I have written, which appear on my LinkedIn page:

ARTICLE—18 (December 13, 2019)

WHERE ARE THE STARS (November 6, 2019)

THE MOST POWERFUL FORM OF LEADERSHIP: MENTORING (September 16, 2019)

UNITED STATES OF AUTHORITARIAN AMERICA (September 11, 2019)

EXTRICATION FROM ALICE'S HOLE (September 5, 2019)

WHAT (really) GOES INTO OPIOID CRISIS THAT WORKS? (March 2, 2019)

AT LAST, THE SECRET TO "WAR ON DRUGS," — A PARA-
DIGM SHIFT IS REVEALED

THE OPIOID CRISIS — PLAN FOR A BETTER INSIGHT
(March 1, 2019)

A JOURNEY FROM THE SHINING SEA (February 25, 2019)

"SEA TO SHINING SEA" — A NATION'S OPIOID CRISIS,
HAVE YOU EVER WONDERED? (February 3, 2019)

"SEA TO SHINING SEA" — AMERICA SUICIDE EPIDEMIC
AND A LOOK FROM THE OTHER SIDE (January 27, 2019)

"SEA TO SHINING SEA" — AMERICA OPIOID EPIDEMIC
AND THE RENAISSANCE (August 13, 2017)

"SEA TO SHINING SEA" — ANOTHER THOUGHT (July 30, 2017)

"SEA TO SHINING SEA" — A NATION'S OPIOID CRISIS!
(July 5, 2017)

CONTINUED THOUGHTS CONCERNING "SEA TO SHIN-
ING SEA" — AMERICA'S OPIOID EPIDEMIC (June 28, 2017)

"SEA TO SHINING SEA" — CONTINUED THOUGHTS ON A
NATION'S OPIOID CRISIS — IT'S COMPLICATED (June 11, 2017)

"SEA TO SHINING SEA" — THOUGHTS ON OUR NATION'S
OPIOID EPIDEMIC (May 25, 2017)

"SEA TO SHINING SEA: THOUGHTS ON OUR NATION'S
OPIOID EPIDEMIC (May 10, 2017)

Professional Experience

SONOMA VALLEY COMMUNITY HEALTH CENTER

05/2019–Present

Integrated Behavioral Health Specialist (IBHS)

At Sonoma Valley Community Health Center (SVCHC) we want
to provide you with comprehensive care for your optimal health.
Often patients see their doctors when care is critical; however, pre-
ventative care is available and is "your pathway to good health." We

offer many programs, from early childhood exams, annual physi-
cals, and cancer prevention screenings to diabetes management to
ensure you have the best health, right now.

PETALUMA FAMILY THERAPY—PRIVATE PRACTICE

Petaluma, California

05/2018–07/2019

Petaluma Family Therapy is a highly respected counseling center
of fully Licensed Marriage and Family Therapists that work with
youth ages 9–17, adults, couples, and families. Passionate about
helping people through their struggles, and believe that connection,
exploration, and courage can change lives.

PROJECT-90 (P-90)

01/2017–04/2018

Volunteer

Provides a 12-step social model recovery program for alcoholic and
drug-abusing men as well as dual diagnosis clients. The program
lasts three months.

IN-HOME SUPPORTIVE SERVICES (IHSS)

01/2016–01/2018

During this period of time, I was the sole caregiver for my mother
who was dealing with severe depression with an underlying issue
with COPD. I was not receiving financial remunerations from the
state and was doing so with my own personal savings.

MENTAL HEALTH NETWORK

04/2009–01/2016

Government Service (MFLC Program)

Responsible as an independent contractor to provide short-
term, non-medical counseling to Special Operations Forces

(SOCOM-SOF), service members, and their families through the Military & Family Life Consultant (MFLC) Program to augment existing military support programs worldwide. Through the MFLC Program, I assisted service members and their families with issues they may have faced through the cycle of deployment—from leaving their loved ones and possibly living and working in harm's way to reintegrating with their community and family. I provided support for a range of issues including: relationships, crisis intervention, stress management, grief, occupational and other individual and family issues. Psycho-educational presentations on reunion/reintegration, stress/coping, grief/loss and deployment were provided to commands, Family Readiness Groups, and Soldier Readiness Processing.

CALIFORNIA STATE PRISON SOLANO—CDCR

Solano, California

12/2007–04/2009

Licensed Clinical Social Worker/ Board Certified Diplomate

Under general direction in a state medical correctional facility or inpatient clinic, conducted responsible psychiatric / medical social work with and on behalf of mentally, physically, or developmentally disabled persons and their relatives; maintained order and supervised the conduct of inmates and/or youthful offenders; protected and maintained the safety of persons and property and other related work.

VETERANS HOME OF YOUNTVILLE

Yountville, California

04/2007–11/2007

Clinical Social Worker

As a Clinical Social Worker of an independent living facility housing 100 retired veterans, the incumbent provided social work services to these individuals and their families primarily in the inpatient setting. In some instances, the incumbent was assigned to specific ambulatory clinics that met weekly to enhance the continuity of care for the specific program. Discharge planning was a major component of the inpatient worker. The incumbent was responsible and accountable for screening 100 percent of admitted patients to their team or program as a member of an interdisciplinary team.

SONOMA DEVELOPMENTAL CENTER

Eldridge, California

02/2006–04/2007

Clinical Social Worker

As a Clinical Social Worker, I secured accurate social data and recorded such data systematically. An essential component was to prepare clear, accurate, and concise reports. Another requirement was working with family and community agencies in preparation for discharge. Finally, it was necessary to analyze situations accurately and take effective action, whether in the form of communicating effectively, providing professional consultation, or developing and implementing programs.

CHILD PROTECTIVE SERVICES

Mariposa, California

09/2022–01/2006

Social Worker

As a social worker, I promoted, restoree, maintained, and enhanced the social functioning of individuals, families, groups, organizations, and communities. Worked under supervision while accumulating required hours for licensure as a Licensed Clinical Social Worker (LCSW).

UNIVERSITY OF CALIFORNIA LOS ANGELES (UCLA)

Los Angeles, California

08/2000–06/2002

Graduate Student

Graduate student in the School of Social Welfare and Public Policy, macro concentration in administrative policy. First year internship at the Los Angeles County Department of Child/Family Services (DCFS); Second year internship spent at Child and Family Guidance Center, clinical perspective.

MILLS-PENINSULA HEALTH SERVICES

Burlingame, California

03/2000–07/2000

Mental Health Worker

Adolescent mental health, adult mental health, and chemical dependency unit mental health worker in the behavioral health department.

RESIDENTIAL TREATMENT OF WEST MICHIGAN, INC.

Grand Rapids, Michigan

07/1998–07/1999

Residential Instructor

Counseled at a community-based licensed 20-bed AFC utilizing individual treatment modalities (personal centered planning, behavior modification plans), for adults with a DSM IV Axis I diagnosis. The majority of current consumers are suffering from various forms of schizophrenia.

SELF-EMPLOYED

07/1996–07/2000

Author

During these three years, I traveled throughout the United States, gathering information for a social commentary describing an adolescent world, its problems, and its possible solutions. Having been accepted by "AmErica House Publishing," the book will be published under the America House logo, in cooperation with PublishAmerica, Inc.

BOYS & GIRLS CLUB OF AMERICA

South San Francisco, California

03/1992–06/1996

Unit Director

Responsible for supervising and training staff, writing reports, proposals, and grants. Developed and controlled budgets while determining community needs through collaboration with community organizations. Initiated new programs and long-range goal planning.

FORENSIC MENTAL HEALTH

Redwood City, California

11/994–06/1995

Volunteer

Provided recovery services to the C.A.S.E. program as a volunteer (Clean And Sober Experience, a 64-bed residential recovery program operated in the Maguire Correctional Facility).

PROJECT NINETY INC.

San Mateo, California

07/1991–07/1992

Weekend Duty Counselor (Adult)

Responsibilities as independent weekend counselor for group and individual counseling. Facilitated alcohol/drug education, intakes, crisis intervention, and outpatient aftercare. Familiarity with 12-step programs. Experience includes dual diagnosed patients.

DAYTOP VILLAGE, INC.

Redwood City, California

03/1989–03/1992

Senior Night Staff Counselor (Adolescent)

Responsible for overnight resident safety, group facilitation, individual counseling, personal recovery planning, exit plan. Facilitated family related education and counseling of drug/ alcohol abuse. Responsible for intakes, case management, crisis intervention, referrals to appropriate community/support services. Facilitate aftercare/outpatient. Coordinated treatment plan with parole, probation, and mental health departments.

HBA BUSINESS PLAN

PHILOSOPHY

The concept of honor is one long-held by upright, virtuous people. Honor is defined by the Webster Dictionary as," integrity in one's beliefs" and as such, Honor Bound Academy's philosophy is grounded in the military code of honor exhibited by members of the Navy SEAL's. Members of a SEAL team embrace the military code of honor, dedication, sacrifice for the greater good and a level of es sprit de corps rarely found in civilian life. Similar to the Navy's motto of, "Not For Self But Country," SEAL's live out a code of brotherhood in which they will give their life so that their brother may live. It is this sense of honor, of loyalty to oneself and the team, of a commitment to excellence that Honor Bound Academy will instill in its students.

CONCEPT/MISSION STATEMENT

Fifty selected males ages 18–20 years old will experience a fully-immersive, 365-day program called Honor Bound Academy based in Sonoma County, CA, where a team consisting of a licensed clinical social worker, volunteer mentors, and staff will expose them to education, experiences, and counseling that will dramatically improve their self-esteem and instill in them a sense of honor. Honor Bound Academy will instill in them a philosophy that they are honor-bound: to themselves, their teammates, and to society as a whole. Through this experience the program's goal is to help these teens develop their internal resources so as to realize their potential, converting potential burdens on society into productive, responsible contributors as mature and socially-responsible men.

THE BUSINESS MODEL

The Service: HBA will provide instruction, training, mentoring and counseling to all of its youth.

The Facility: HBA will occupy a large residential facility located within extensive grounds in a rural setting in Northern California within a 3-hour drive of the San Francisco Bay Area. The program will involve extensive travel and activity beyond this facility.

The Team: HBA will utilize paid staff and volunteers with training in producing highly-motivated, disciplined, responsible, effective young men.

The Clients: "Clients" is defined as the youths enrolled in the program. HBA will recruit and screen candidates nominated by concerned families, social workers, health professionals, juvenile justice programs, and parents.

The Customers: "Customers" is defined as private individuals contributed to the program with financial and/or logistical support. At this time HBA seeks to be funded solely by private donors "Patron's" and not any governmental programs/grants.

THE ORGANIZATION

The organization will consist of the Program Director, eight additional faculty, and a facility manager/housekeeper/cook. A part-time instructor in physical and mental disciplines (yoga instructor) will be employed, as well as the paid services of a part-time psychologist. Several volunteer mentors (retired US Navy SEALS) will complete the team. Mr. LaGrave will supervise the other 8 faculty members, each experienced in personal development programs that require and drive the cognitive, physical and character formation of its clients, and will be advised by an advisory board.

THE INDUSTRY/COMPETITORS

Honor Bound Academy is unlike any other type of program of its kind in existence. There are a number of programs for youth: boot camps, therapeutic boarding schools, military schools, and wilderness schools. Institutions with various mixes of therapy, academics, outdoor challenges, schedule discipline, and physical rigor. Some accept clients from both public and private customers, some accept only private clients. There are over 40 such facilities for "dependent and delinquent youth" throughout Sonoma County and approximately five group homes in nearby Marin County. (1) The purpose of these sites is wide-ranging and includes services to youth needing developmental assistance, specialized education, and substance abuse treatment. These sites cater to youth between 12 and 18 years of age and not the HBA's target group. Youth correctional facilities and conservation camps are widely absent from the market area (Sonoma County and surrounding Bay Area counties). The nearest youth correctional facilities are located in Stockton and Folsom, California, approximately 100 miles to the east. As of August 2009, no requests from counties in the target area were submitted to develop community re-entry facilities through Assembly Bill 900. A cursory review yielded no local, specialized residential facilities serving men 18-20 years of age who are transitioning back into their communities.

Competition for clients will come from both private and public institutions. A number of private therapeutic boarding schools and most counties and states have juvenile justice, mental health and substance abuse programs that deal with the same element of the population as does HBA. Given the absence of a predecessor, Honor Bound Academy does not yet have a program with which to compare its standards. Among group homes, the Office of Juvenile Justice and Delinquency Prevention (OJJDP) identifies Boys'Town and VisionQuest as model programs based on research indicating that participants were less likely to be rearrested than youth who did not participate in the programs. The OJJDP identifies VisionQuest and the East Texas Experiential Learning Center as model wilderness camp programs for their impact on recidivism. Honor Bound Academy would be an innovative program that reflects aspects of these and other program designs; thus, the "gold standard" for such a program has not yet been established.

Description

The industry, broadly described as therapeutic boarding schools, encompasses institutions and programs that may variously emphasize clinical therapy, behavioral modification, adventure survival, and military-style discipline. It delivers services to a clientele characterized by some combination of anti-social or criminal behavior, substance abuse, academic under-performance, and/or family discord. Unlike short-term boot camps, these programs are longer-term and are typically more long-lasting in their effect.

Through their discussion of intervention and prevention programs required to improve youths' likelihood of future achievement, the Office of Juvenile Justice and Delinquency Prevention (OJJDP) identifies youths' needs for focused attention to physical, educational, psychological and vocational development. The OJJDP offers an inventory of over 20 types of programs that address these needs and their characteristics of model programs. The services similar to those to be offered by HBA are:

Academic Skills Enhancement

Aftercare

After School/Recreation

Classroom Curricula

Cognitive Behavior Treatment

Conflict Resolution/Interpersonal Skills

Group Home

Leadership and Youth Development

Restorative Justice

Wilderness Camps

Growth Rate

Although precise numbers are not available, the industry and its potential clientele are growing faster than the national population largely because of changes in family and community structures and increased awareness of methods for dealing with juvenile delinquency, substance abuse, anti-social behavior, and youth in general.

Regulation and Certification

Authorities: Institutions with a mission similar to HBA's may fall within the purview of the state Dept. of Social Services, the Dept. of Education and the Juvenile Justice System.

Licenses, Certifications and Permits: HBA may require a Community Care License, a state Charter for the school, a certification from an Alliance of Child and Family Services or similar organization, a certification from the juvenile justice authorities, a permit from the county for property use consistent with the zoning of the subject property, and approvals from the local building inspector, Fire Marshall and water quality authority.

COMPETITIVE POSITION

HBA's unique combination of elements utilizing therapeutic methods, military structure and discipline, psychological and traditional spiritual elements as well as travel and intense physical demands will appeal to potential clients and their parents. Honor Bound Academy mission is distinctive in its proposed clientele and services. Given the narrow age range of the target population (18-20 years), young men will receive more focused attention on pro-social behavior development and personal life skills.

While academic preparation is not the sole focus of Honor Bound Academy, it remains important to maximizing youths' opportunities at later successes, and they will prepare for higher education as a component of the program. However, the academic program at HBA will be distinct from traditional curriculums; young men will participate in a system of learning that they would not otherwise receive post-release. Similar to group homes, Honor Bound Academy will provide structure, including a daily schedule of responsibilities and activities, as well as staff who are appropriately trained to work with the young men. The program will foster personal development—particularly accountability, strength, and adaptability.

HBA's program is unique in its methods and anticipated outcomes. The program is developed to resolve deficiencies in education and personal development and bolster young men's capacities to be responsible, honorable adults. The method by which this is done begins with enabling youth to understand their respective histories and abilities so as to better map their future potential. Youth will receive lessons about the sciences, biology, genealogy, and human development, nature, religion and myth, history, and institutions as these topics relate to their lives and environments. Programming evolves to include rigorous physical activity that is only successful when youth are equally accountable for themselves and each other. HBA clients will focus daily on self-reflection, personal distress, and restorative justice planning during daily, individual therapy sessions led by Director LaGrave. These program components are designed to enhance young men's likelihood of positive outcomes, outlined in the attached program model.

HBA is unique within its marketplace by virtue of its combination of physical and spiritual disciplines, emphasis on developing psychological and physiological strength and a sense of personal honor and team consciousness and the rigor of its US Navy SEAL-inspired programs. HBA's program is distinguished by its combination of elements of emotional growth and adventure-therapy programs with the discipline of elite military training.

Beyond the set of customary services provided in state-funded facilities such as basic education, counseling and therapy, as well as vocational training, Honor Bound Academy offers programming that was previously unavailable. A critical part of programming is grounded in rite-of-passage instruction—an integrated system of curricula, rigorous physical activity, wilderness exploration, and therapy—intended to transition youth into adulthood. The curriculum is designed to develop adaptability, physical fitness, leadership, experiential learning, and honor among its students. Existing facilities and programs for the targeted youth do not replicate Honor Bound Academy. Group homes, for example, are often seen as the last step before, or one step following, incarceration. Youth receive focused care, counseling and education while in these homes. However, services are largely intervention to redirect youths' paths from incarceration or re-incarceration, not to transition young adults (ages 18–20) into adulthood and their communities. Similarly, correctional facilities—designed to limit youths' movement—and day or residential treatment centers for mental health and substance abuse care do not reflect the mission, or aspire to the goals of, Honor Bound Academy.

Identifying Clients (Youths)

Clients proposed by potential customers will, before acceptance into HBA, undergo thorough screening to determine if they can meet the mental and physical requirements of the program, can commit to its discipline, and indicate a reasonable expectation of success from the program.

Existing research identifies a lengthy inventory of risk factors related to delinquency, factors that are innate to the youth (compared to risk factors in their environments) and include cognitive challenges (i.e., defiance, aggression, lack of self-restraint, high sensation-seeking, limited responsibility development, limited foresight of consequences, limited identity development, poor self-assessment, poor educational performance, drug use, and troubled interpersonal relationships, among other correlates and predictors that researchers continue to identify).

The vast number of potential clients (recipients of the services) for the HBA program can come from several sources, among them being the California Department of Corrections and Rehabilitation (CDCR). Although statistics vary across data sources and jurisdictions (i.e., the Federal Bureau of Investigation, United States Department of Justice, state departments, independent research entities), the (CDCR) estimated that 166,569 persons were incarcerated in their facilities by August 2009. The Division of Juvenile Justice (DJJ), previously known as the California Youth Authority, was responsible for the 1,870 youth in their institutions and 2,078 youth on parole. The CDCR and DJJ have authority over juvenile cases—those involving persons no older than 21 years of age—however statistics indicate that the preponderance of cases is within DJJ purview. Ninety-five percent of 2008 DJJ cases (1,496) and 96% of 2008 CDCR cases (130) were young men, and 55% of total cases were between 18 and 20 years of age. Eleven percent (179) of all young men within CDCR and DJJ jurisdictions were committed in Bay Area counties (2). Thus we estimate that as many as 200 young men may be eligible for consideration for acceptance into HBA's 50 available slots. This is just one among several potential sources for clients.

SELLING TO THE CLIENTS (PARENTS & YOUTHS)

The parents of potential clients will be addressed through the website, membership and listing in the national associations, and personal presentation to consultants specializing in the placement of troubled youth. Proposed clients will be presented with an outline of the program and its expectations from and for the client. Its level of rigor and required commitment will be stressed. Every troubled boy is not a feasible candidate for this position.

Applicants will be screened thoroughly including personal interviews and interviews with parents, social workers and parole officers, and reviews of records and recommendations. Proposed clients will be presented with an outline of the program and its expectations from and for the client. Its level of rigor and required commitment will be stressed. Every troubled boy is not a feasible candidate for this position.

PROMOTION TO THE CUSTOMERS (PRIVATE DONORS)

The HBA program will be promoted to the public sector potential customers by personal meetings and presentations by the Director.

NUMBER OF CLIENTS

The initial pilot program with 50 clients will be expanded the following year to 100 (including student mentors from the previous class).

Following the successful establishment and operation of the Academy's pilot program, it is the intent to open sites in other regions. Information found earlier through the section: Patron's, Native American people's including geographical location, a Special Forces foundation, and structures found in the "Silmarillion."

COST TO CLIENTS

It is recognized that the families of prospective clients will most often not be able or willing to cover the costs of the program. All costs associated by the program will be covered by financial resources provided by the customers (private donors). There will be no cost to the parents.

MANAGEMENT

Leadership

HBA will be managed by the Director, Tom LaGrave M.S.W., L.C.S.W who, for over 30 years, has been responsible for the physical and psychological health, for the socialization and personal development, of adolescents and young men and their families in clinical, juvenile justice, mental health, hospital, residential, and military settings. Mr. LaGrave, a Licensed Clinical Social Worker, is known for his work with youthful offenders, adolescent chemical dependency, psychological/social family counseling, youth program development and training, and coordination of remediation and treatment programs with juvenile justice and mental health programs. In addition to his training as U.S. Navy Hospital Corpsman and as a US Navy SEAL, he holds a Master's Degree in Social Work from UCLA and a degree in Business Administration from Cornerstone University. (please see Appendix A for full resume).

Advisement/Governance

The Director will be advised by an Advisory Board composed of legal, financial, business, psychological, social work and juvenile justice professionals that will provide consultation, direction and review for the HBA team and its programs.

LOCATION

Region

Honor Bound Academy will be located in rural Sonoma or Mendocino County, CA.

Site

The HBA facility will be sited for access to sufficient acreage for outdoor exercises (minimum of 25 acres).

DEVELOPMENT STAGE

HBA is in the early stages of development.

Strategic Vision: Completed

Business Plan: Completed

Team: Core assembled (Director, full-time assistants, volunteer mentors)

Region: Selected

Site: Requirements identified, exact site TBD

Permits: To be acquired

Funding: To be acquired

Current Financial Status

The Founder is now seeking funding to cover start-up costs and two years of operations ($6,370,000). Funding for start-up will be sought by the Director from individual private donors. The Director has obtained seed capital to support the original solicitation and acquisition of funding for start-up and operations.

Customer Service

Customers (donors) will receive regular Director's Reports, based on program logs and staff journals, outlining the activity, issues, and accomplishments. The parents of the clients will receive regular updates as well and alerted to any major issues regarding their son.

Facilities

Location: HBA will be located in rural Sonoma County or Mendocino County, CA.

Lease: Unless the property is purchased it is anticipated that the lease rate will be approximately $ 20,000/ mo.

Improvements: The site will include residential accommodations for 100+ clients plus 8 full-time faculty and one administrative staff, as well as buildings for a classroom and for equipment storage.

Utilities: In addition to water, sewage, gas, electric, and telephone service, HBA will have high-speed internet service installed.

Maintenance: Building and grounds maintenance will be handled by the clients and staff under the guidance of professionals, as required.

Equipment: Computing, classroom and office equipment will be purchased, as will tools for building and grounds maintenance. Outdoor equipment for land-based and water-based exercises will also be acquired.

Furnishings: Household, office and classroom furnishings will be acquired. As often as possible, donations in kind will be sought.

Vehicles: three 10-passenger vans will be leased, along with 2–40 seat Buses.

HBA CURRICULUM

See Honor Bound Academy Strategic Vision

TECHNOLOGY EMPLOYED

The program will give clients access to, and instruction on, computers and the internet. In the water-based exercises, proven gear for underwater activity and survival will be utilized. For land-based wilderness exercises, high-performance, lightweight gear will be acquired.

STAFFING

Instructional Staff

The Director and 8 other full-time faculty members as well as 1 part-time instructor will comprise the academic staff.

Support Staff

A full-time housekeeper will be employed. A part-time yoga instructor will be utilized, as well as a part-time licensed Psychologist (PhD).

Skills and Experience

The eight designated faculty members are former US Navy SEAL's. The Director, a Licensed Social Worker, has 30 years of experience in dealing with the behavioral and health problems of young men. (See full biography/qualifications of Director in the Strategic Vision).

Additional Instructional Staff

With the increase of participants in the second year, it will be necessary to add four (4) new full-time faculty members.

Payroll

The annual payroll first year is projected to be $1,449,500. The annual payroll second year is projected to be $1,449,500.

FINANCIAL CONTROLS

HBA will secure the services of a Certified Public Accountant to install appropriate financial controls.

REGULATORY COMPLIANCE

Zoning: A Conditional Use Permit will be obtained from the County, consistent with the zoning of the site.

Certification: HBA will obtain certification from the California Department of Education and from the County. Certification will also be sought from the California Alliance of Child and Family Services.

Licensing: A Community Care License from the California Department of Social Services will be required to house the minor dependents up to age 20.

Occupancy Permits: Occupancy permits will be obtained from the County.

Management and Organization

Structure: All faculty, staff and consultants will report to the Director. The Director will be guided by the Advisory Board, will work closely with the CPA, and provide informational reports to the customers (donors).

Style: The management style will be collegial, with an informal military flavor.

Compensation

Management: The Director will receive an annual salary of $175,000.

Staff: The other two faculty members' annual salary will be $100,000, each. The housekeeper/cook/facility manager will receive $55,000/yr. The part-time yoga/meditation instructor will be paid $20,000/year and the part-time Psychologist will be paid 65,000/yr.

Other: The CPA will be paid an hourly rate and approximate costs are covered in the Financials under Misc. expenses.

Second Year Staffing: With full implementation of 100 participants (50—year one, 50—additional year two), four supplementary paid faculty members are required. The other four faculty members' annual salary will be $100,000, each.

Financials

HONOR BOUND ACADEMY FINANCIAL STATEMENT

SALARY AND BENEFITS:	Year 1	Year 2	2 Year Totals
Director's Salary	$ 175,000	$ 175,000	
Professional Staff Salaries (8)	$ 800,000	$ 800,000	
Part-time Staff Salaries (2) (psychologist/yoga) (65/20)	$ 85,000	$ 85,000	
Part-time Staff Salaries	$ 55,000	$ 55,000	
Total Salaries:	$ 1,115,000	$ 1,115,000	$ 2,230,000
Benefits (30% of salaries)	$ 334,500	$ 334,500	$ 669,000
	$ 1,449,500	$ 1,449,500	$ 2,899,000
SERVICES AND SUPPLIES:			
Mortgage Payment and Maintenance	$ 250,000	$ 250,000	
Vehicle Rental (3)	$ 23,000	$ 23,000	
Vehicle Operation and Maintenance	$ 15,000	$ 15,000	
Utilities	$ 10,000	$ 10,000	
Communications	$ 10,000	$ 10,000	
Office and school supplies	$ 15,000	$ 15,000	
Insurance	$ 75,000	$ 75,000	
Professional Fees	$ 25,000	$ 25,000	
Licensing and Certification Fees	$ 25,000	$ 25,000	
Fundraising Expenses	$ 100,000	$ 100,000	
Miscellaneous	$ 50,000	$ 50,000	
	$ 598,000	$ 598,000	$ 1,196,000
PROGRAM EXPENSES:			
Teaching Materials	$ 25,000	$ 25,000	
Uniforms	$ 65,000	$ 65,000	
Food	$ 125,000	$ 125,000	
Equipment Repair and Replacement	$ 55,000	$ 55,000	
Regional Travel and International Travel	$ 280,000	$ 280,000	
Outdoor Training Fees	$ 60,000	$ 60,000	
Miscellaneous	$ 50,000	$ 50,000	
Mentors' Expenses	$ 55,000	$ 55,000	
	$ 715,000	$ 715,000	$ 1,430,000
TOTAL OPERATING EXPENSES:	**$ 2,762,500**	**$ 2,762,500**	**$ 5,525,000**

BUDGET DETAIL:

	Year 1	Year 2	2 Year Totals
Salary and Benefits	$ 1,449,500	$ 1,449,500	
Services and Supplies	$ 598,000	$ 598,000	
Program Expenses	$ 715,000	$ 715,000	
	$ 2,762,500	$ 2,762,500	$ 5,525,000

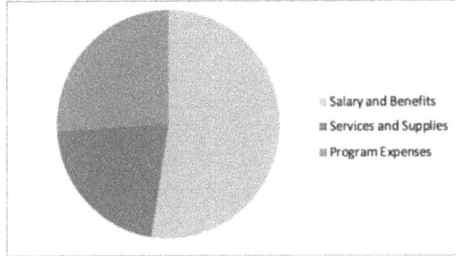

- Salary and Benefits
- Services and Supplies
- Program Expenses

CAPITAL AND ONE TIME EXPENDITURES:

Down Payment on Property	$ 250,000	
Tenant Improvements	$ 120,000	
Computing & Communications Equipment	$ 100,000	
Classroom Furnishings	$ 35,000	
Residential Furnishings	$ 75,000	
Classroom Materials and Resources	$ 90,000	
Outdoor Equipment	$ 100,000	
Miscellaneous	$ 75,000	
	$ 845,000	$ 845,000

FUNDS REQUIRED FOR STARTUP AND 2 YEARS OF OPERATION:

Year 1	Year 2	2 Year Totals
$ 3,607,500	$ 2,762,500	$ 6,370,000

BIBLIOGRAPHY

"To Benjamin Franklin from Thomas Jefferson, [21 June 1776?]," Founders Online, National Archives, *https://founders.archives.gov/documents/Franklin/01-22-02-0284.* [Original source: *The Papers of Benjamin Franklin*, vol. 22, March 23, 1775, through October 27, 1776, ed. William B. Willcox. New Haven and London: Yale University Press, 1982, pp. 485–486.]. Accessed 31 Mar 2024.

160th Special Operations Aviation Regiment (Airborne). *https://en.wikipedia.org/wiki/160th_Special_Operations_Aviation_Regiment_(Airborne)*: accessed 5 Feb 2020.

Addison, II, L.C., The Tenets of Freemasonry: Mere Words or Good Guidelines? *https://grandlodgeofiowa.org/docs/Philosophy_Masonry/TheTenetsOfFreemasonry.pdf*: accessed 1 Apr 2024.

Age of Aquarius *https://en.wikipedia.org/wiki/Age_of_Aquarius#:~:text=According%20to%20various%20astrologers'%20calculations,if%20it%20has%20already%20started*: accessed 2 Apr 2024.

American Board of Examiners in Clinical Social Work (ABE). *https://www.socialworkdegreeguide.com/faq/what-is-the-american-board-of-examiners-in-clinical-social-work/*: accessed 31 Mar 2024.

Arthur Conan Doyle Quotes. BrainyQuote.com, BrainyMedia Inc, 2024. *https://www.brainyquote.com/quotes/arthur_conan_doyle_134512*: accessed 31 Mar 2024.

Assange, Julian. *https://en.wikipedia.org/wiki/Julian_Assange*: accessed 2 Apr 2024.

Baby Boomers. *https://en.wikipedia.org/wiki/Baby_boomers*: accessed 1 Apr 2024.

Belegost. *https://tolkiengateway.net/wiki/Belegost*: accessed 7 Apr 2024.

Bezos, Jeff. *https://en.wikipedia.org/wiki/Jeff_Bezos*: accessed 7 Apr 2024.

Black Lives Matter (BLM). *https://en.wikipedia.org/wiki/Black_Lives_Matter*: accessed 1 Apr 2024.

Bloomberg, Michael. *https://en.wikipedia.org/wiki/Michael_Bloomberg*: accessed 7 Apr 2024.

Boys & Girls Clubs of America, National Headquarters, *https://www.bgca.org/about-us/contact-us/*: accessed 31 Mar 2024.

Boys & Girls Clubs of America. *https://www.bgca.org/about-us/*: accessed 31 Mar 2024.

Brin, Sergey. *https://en.wikipedia.org/wiki/Sergey_Brin*: accessed 7 Apr 2024.

Buffett, Warren. *https://en.wikipedia.org/wiki/Warren_Buffett*: accessed 7 Apr 2024.

Campbell, Joseph. *https://www.goodreads.com/quotes/143093-follow-your-bliss-if-you-do-follow-your-bliss-you*: accessed 31 Mar 2024.

Cherokee Nation. *https://en.wikipedia.org/wiki/Cherokee_Nation*: accessed 11 Aug 2020.

Comanche. *https://en.wikipedia.org/wiki/Comanche*: accessed 4 Jun 2020.

Cousineau, Phil, Editor, *The Hero's Journey: Joseph Campbell on His Life and Work (The Collected Works of Joseph Campbell)*, (Novato, California: New World Library, 2003).

Daytop Village, Adolescent Recovery Facility located in Woodside, California. *https://www.drug-rehab-headquarters.com/california/facility/daytop-village-inc-redwood-city/*: accessed 31 Mar 2024.

Ellis, David, The Psychology of Mystery. *https://www.donweaver.org/the-psychology-of-mystery/*: accessed 1 Apr 2024.

Ellison, Larry. *https://en.wikipedia.org/wiki/Larry_Ellison*: accessed 7 Apr 2024.

Epictetus Quotes. BrainyQuote.com, BrainyMedia Inc, 2024. *https://www.brainyquote.com/quotes/epictetus_106298*: accessed 2 Apr 2024.

Follow Your Bliss, Joseph Campbell Foundation *https://www.jcf.org/learn/joseph-campbell-follow-your-bliss*: accessed 31 Mar 2024.

Gates, Bill. *https://en.wikipedia.org/wiki/Bill_Gates*: accessed 7 Apr 2024.

Generation Alpha. *https://en.wikipedia.org/wiki/Generation_Alpha*: accessed 1 Apr 2024.

Generation X. *https://en.wikipedia.org/wiki/Generation_X*: accessed 1 Apr 2024.

Generation Z. *https://en.wikipedia.org/wiki/Generation_Z*: accessed 1 Apr 2024.

Get Smarter with edX, The Strengths and Weaknesses of Every Generation in your Workforce *https://www.getsmarter.com/blog/career-advice/know-your-generationals/*: accessed 2 Jul 2020.

Gondolin. *https://en.wikipedia.org/wiki/Gondolin*: accessed 5 Nov 2023.

Grand Traverse Band of Ottawa and Chippewa Indians. *https://en.wikipedia.org/wiki/Grand_Traverse_Band_of_Ottawa_and_Chippewa_Indians*: accessed 4 Jun 2020.

Greatest Generation. *https://en.wikipedia.org/wiki/Greatest_Generation*: accessed 1 Apr 2024.

Grey Havens. *https://tolkiengateway.net/wiki/Grey_Havens*: accessed 7 Apr 2024.

Griffith, Samuel B. *The Illustrated Art of War*. 2005. Oxford University Press. *https://en.wikipedia.org/wiki/The_Art_of_War*: accessed 1 Apr 2024.

Icahn, Carl. *https://en.wikipedia.org/wiki/Carl_Icahn*: accessed 7 Apr 2024.

ICIJ (International Consortium of Investigative Journalists. *https://www.icij.org/*: accessed 2 Apr 2024.

Inuit. *https://en.wikipedia.org/wiki/Inuit*: accessed 4 Jun 2020.

Iroquois. *https://en.wikipedia.org/wiki/Iroquois*: accessed 16 Jun 2020.

Isengard. *https://en.wikipedia.org/wiki/Isengard*: accessed 5 Nov 2023.

Joint Special Operations Command. *https://en.wikipedia.org/wiki/Joint_Special_Operations_Command*: accessed 5 Jun 2020.

Jung, Carl G., John Jung, M. L. von Franz, Editors, *Man and His Symbols* (London, United Kingdom: Aldus Books Ltd., 1971).

Knight, Phil. *https://en.wikipedia.org/wiki/Phil_Knight*: accessed 7 Apr 2024.

LaGrave, Tom. "Honor Bound Academy." *https://thehonorboundacademy.org/*: accessed 31 Mar 2024.

Lakota People. *https://en.wikipedia.org/wiki/Lakota_people*: accessed 7 Apr 2024.

Led Zeppelin; Songwriters-Jimmy Page, John Bonham, John Paul Jones, Robert Anthony Plant, "Good Times Bad Times," Warner Chappell Music, Inc., 1969. *https://lyrics.lyricfind.com/lyrics/led-zeppelin-good-times-bad-times-1*: accessed 1 Apr 2024.

Linkedin. *https://www.linkedin.com/in/tjlagravejr*: accessed 7 Apr 2024.

Linkedin. *https://www.linkedin.com/pulse/adolescent-combat-diplomate tom-lagrave-1e?trk=pulse-article_more-articles_related-content-card*: accessed 8 Apr 2024.

Linkedin. *https://www.linkedin.com/pulse/adolescent-combat-diplomate-tom-lagrave-6c?trk=articles_directory*: accessed 8 Apr 2024.

Linkedin. *https://www.linkedin.com/pulse/adolescent-combat-diplomate-tom-lagrave-9c*: accessed 9 Apr 2024.

Live, Laugh, Love. *https://en.wikipedia.org/wiki/Live,_Laugh,_Love*: accessed 31 Mar 2024.

Lotr-The Gray Havens-Watchtower. https://ideas.lego.com/projects. (excerpt from *http://lotr.wikia.com*): accessed 9 Apr 2024.

Masonic Ritual and Symbolism. *https://en.wikipedia.org/wiki/Masonic_ritual_and_symbolism*: accessed 31 Mar 2024.

Me Too Movement. *https://en.wikipedia.org/wiki/MeToo_movement*: accessed 1 Apr 2024.

Menegroth. *https://tolkiengateway.net/wiki/Menegroth*: accessed 5 Nov 2023.

Mental Health Network Government Services (MHNGS). *http://www.nationalresourcedirectory.gov/resource/detail/8765448/MHN+Government+Services+Behavioral+Health+Solutions*: accessed 31 Mar 2024.

Merriam-Webster.com Dictionary, *Merriam-Webster*. "Precept." (*https://www.merriam-webster.com/dictionary/precept*): accessed 31 Mar 2024.

Merriam-Webster.com Dictionary, *Merriam-Webster,* "Ruthless." *https://www
.merriam-webster.com/dictionary/ruthless*: accessed 8 Apr. 2024.

Military–Industrial Complex (MIC). *https://en.wikipedia.org/wiki/Military
%E2%80%93industrial_complex*: accessed 1 Apr 2024.

Millennials. *https://en.wikipedia.org/wiki/Millennials*: accessed 1 Apr 2024.

Minas Tirith. *https://en.wikipedia.org/wiki/Minas_Tirith*: accessed 5 Nov 2023.

Moria, Middle Earth. *https://en.wikipedia.org/wiki/Moria,_Middle-earth*: accessed
21 Oct 2023.

Musk, Elon. *https://en.wikipedia.org/wiki/Elon_Musk*: accessed 7 Apr 2024.

Nargothrond. *https://thetolkien.forum/wiki/Nargothrond*: accessed 1 Apr 2024.

Natchez People. *https://en.wikipedia.org/wiki/Natchez_people*: accessed 4 Jun 2020.

Navajo. *https://en.wikipedia.org/wiki/Navajo*: accessed 4 Jun 2020.

Navy SEAL & RECON Special Operations Combat Medic Technician (NEC 8492),
Navy Medicine, *https://www.med.navy.mil/Navy-Medicine-Operational-Training
-Command/Naval-Special-Operations-Medical-Institute/Special-Operations-Combat
-Medical-Skills-Sustainment-Course/*, accessed 31 Mar 2024.

New Mexico. *https://en.wikipedia.org/wiki/New_Mexico*: accessed 8 Apr 2024.

Nez Perce. *https://en.wikipedia.org/wiki/Nez_Perce*: accessed 16 Jun 2020.

Nogrod. *http://thetolkienwiki.org/wiki.cgi?Nogrod*: accessed 1 Apr 2023.

Occam's Razor, *https://www.goodreads.com/author/quotes/85818.William_of
_Ockham: accessed 31 Mar 2024.*

Operation Eagle Claw. *https://en.wikipedia.org/wiki/Operation_Eagle_Claw*:
accessed 8 Apr 2024.

Oz, Frank: Yoda. *https://www.imdb.com/title/tt0080684/characters/nm0000568*:
accessed 31 Mar 2024.

Page, Larry. *https://en.wikipedia.org/wiki/Larry_Page*: accessed 7 Apr 2024.

Panama Papers. *https://en.wikipedia.org/wiki/Panama_Papers*: accessed 2 Apr 2024.

Parker, Kim and Rugh Igielnik, Pew Research Center, *On the Cusp of Adulthood
and Facing an Uncertain Future: What We Know About Gen Z So Far,* 14 May
2020. *https://www.pewresearch.org/social-trends/2020/05/14/on-the-cusp-of-
adulthood-and-facing-an-uncertain-future-what-we-know-about-gen-z-so-far-2/*:
accessed 2 Apr 2024.

Pollak, Lindsey. *https://lindseypollak.com/gen-x-the-forgotten-middle-child-is-it-any-
wonder-that-our-theme-song-is-dont-you-forget-about-me/*: accessed 2 Apr 2024.

Private Military Company (PMC); Private Military and Security Company
(PMSC). *https://en.wikipedia.org/wiki/Private_military_company*: accessed 1
Apr 2024.

Project Ninety, San Mateo County, California known as CAMINAR. *https://
www.caminar.org/p90*: accessed 31 Mar 2024.

Rivendell. *https://en.wikipedia.org/wiki/Rivendell*: accessed 1 Apr 2024.

Schleifstein, Darcy, Zachary Dougherty, and Sarah Emily Baum, *"Dear National Rifle Association: We Won't Let You Win. From, Teenagers,"* New York Times, 13 Mar 2018. *https://www.nytimes.com/2018/03/13/opinion/nra-shooting-marjory-stoneman-douglas.html*: accessed 2 Apr 2024.

Seminole. *https://en.wikipedia.org/wiki/Seminole*: accessed 4 Jun 2020.

Silent Generation (*https://en.wikipedia.org/wiki/Silent_Generation*): accessed 1 Apr 2024.

Smith, Scott. "Psychology: A Sense of Mystery May Be the Spice of Life," Capital Gazette, 6 Feb 2014, HTML edition. *https://www.capitalgazette.com/2014/02/06/psychology-a-sense-of-mystery-may-be-the-spice-of-life/*: accessed 1 Apr 2024.

Snowden, Edward. *https://en.wikipedia.org/wiki/Edward_Snowden*: accessed 2 Apr 2024.

Special Operations Forces. *https://www.military.com/special-operations*: accessed 1 Apr 2024.

Special Warfare Insignia, Navy Enlisted Classification (NEC) 5326 Combatant Swimmer (SEAL), *https://en.wikipedia.org/wiki/Special_Warfare_insignia*: accessed 31 Mar 2024.

The Lamentation of the Overflowing Heart of the Red Man of the Forest. http://www.nanations.com/ottawachippewa/lamentation.htm: accessed 9 Apr 2024.

The Medal of Honor. *https://www.cmohs.org/medal*: accessed 31 Mar 2024.

The Pacific Coast Trail (PCT). *https://www.fs.usda.gov/pct/*: accessed 31 Mar 2024.

The Twenty-one Precepts or Moral Commandments of the Ottawa and Chippewa Indians. https://www.nanations.com/ottawachippewa/twenty-oneprecepts.htm: accessed 9 April 2024.

Theodore Roosevelt Conservation Partnership. *https://www.trcp.org/2011/01/18/it-is-not-the-critic-who-counts/*: accessed 31 Mar 2024.

Tír na nÓg. *https://en.wikipedia.org/wiki/T%C3%ADr_na_n%C3%93g#:~:-text=In%20Irish%20mythology%2C%20T%C3%ADr%20na,tale%20of%20Ois%C3%ADn%20and%20Niamh*. Accessed 8 Apr 2024.

Tolkien, J. R. R. *The Silmarillion: The legendary precursor to The Lord of the Rings.* New York, New York: Del Ray Publishing (an imprint of Penguin Random House), 2002.

Tracey B., *This is the dawning of the age of Aquarius. https://thelifestyleconcept.co.uk/blog/this-is-nearly-the-dawning-of-the-age-of-aquarius/*: accessed 2 Apr 2024.

Tzu, Sun. *https://en.wikipedia.org/wiki/Sun_Tzu*: accessed 1 Apr 2024.

Tzu, Sun. *The Art of War* (China, 5th Century BC (Library of Congress Class U101 .S95). *https://en.wikipedia.org/wiki/The_Art_of_War*: accessed 1 Apr 2024.

U.S. Air Force Doctrine. *https://www.doctrine.af.mil/Doctrine-Publications/AFDP -3-50-Personnel-Recovery/*: accessed 8 Apr 2024.

U.S. Department of the Treasury (TARP). *https://home.treasury.gov/data/troubled -asset-relief-program*: accessed 2 Apr 2024.

United States Air Force Combat Control Team. *https://en.wikipedia.org/wiki/ United_States_Air_Force_Combat_Control_Team*: accessed 5 Jun 2020.

United States Air Force Pararescue. *https://en.wikipedia.org/wiki/United_States _Air_Force_Pararescue*: accessed 17 Jun 2020.

United States Air Force Special Reconnaissance. *https://en.wikipedia.org/wiki/ United_States_Air_Force_Special_Reconnaissance*: accessed21 Oct 2023.

United States Army Rangers. *https://en.wikipedia.org/wiki/United_States_Army _Rangers*: accessed 17 Jun 2020.

United States Army Special Forces (SF). *https://en.wikipedia.org/wiki/United_ States_Army_Special_Forces*: accessed 17 Jun 2020.

United States Marine Forces Special Operations Command (MARSOC). *https:// en.wikipedia.org/wiki/United_States_Marine_Forces_Special_Operations _Command*: accessed 10 Aug 2020.

United States Navy SEALs. *https://en.wikipedia.org/wiki/United_States_Navy _SEALs*: accessed 15 Jul 2020.

Velikovsky Reconsidered. Et al. Pensee Editors. New York: Doubleday Publishing, 1976.

Vincit qui se vincit. *https://dribbble.com/shots/5971922-Vincit-qui-se-vincit#*: accessed 1 Apr 2024.

Walk in beauty is the translation of the Navajo term for the spiritual path of celebrating the sacredness of life. https://www.walk-in-beauty.org/: accessed 8 Apr 2024.

Washington Post. *https://www.washingtonpost.com/*: accessed 8 Apr 2024.

Zuckerberg, Mark. *https://en.wikipedia.org/wiki/Mark_Zuckerberg*: accessed 7 Apr 2024.

ENDNOTES

CHAPTER ONE: A GIFT GIVEN

[1] LaGrave, Tom, *Honor Bound Academy* (*https://thehonorboundacademy.org/*): accessed 31 Mar 2024.

[2] Ibid.

[3] Ibid.

[4] Ibid.

[5] Ibid.

[6] Ibid.

CHAPTER TWO: SHIFTING PERSPECTIVE

[7] Ibid.

[8] Ibid.

[9] "Precept." Merriam-Webster.com Dictionary, Merriam-Webster (*https://www.merriam-webster.com/dictionary/precept*): accessed 31 Mar. 2024.

[10] Occam's Razor, *https://www.goodreads.com/author/quotes/85818.William_of_Ockham*, accessed 31 Mar. 2024.

[11] Arthur Conan Doyle Quotes. BrainyQuote.com, BrainyMedia Inc, 2024. *https://www.brainyquote.com/quotes/arthur_conan_doyle_134512* , accessed March 31, 2024.

[12] Frank Oz: Yoda. *https://www.imdb.com/title/tt0080684/characters/nm0000568*, accessed 31 Mar 2024.

[13] LaGrave, "Honor Bound Academy" (*https://thehonorboundacademy.org/*): accessed 31 Mar 2024.

[14] Joseph Campbell. *https://www.goodreads.com/quotes/143093-follow-your-bliss-if-you-do-follow-your-bliss-you*, accessed 31 Mar 2024.

[15] Theodore Roosevelt Conservation Partnership, *https://www.trcp.org/2011/01/18/it-is-not-the-critic-who-counts/*, accessed 31 Mar 2024.

CHAPTER THREE: PATTERNS FROM THE PAST

[16] Project Ninety in San Mateo County, California is now known as CAMINAR. Since 1972, Project Ninety has served individuals, families and the Bay Area community through its residential alcohol and substance abuse treatment services. What began as a humble idea has grown into a premier human services organization. *https://www.caminar.org/p90*, accessed 31 Mar 2024.

[17] Daytop Village was an adolescent recovery facility located in Woodside, California.

[18] Boys & Girls Clubs of America's Mission is "To enable all young people, especially those who need us most, to reach their full potential as productive, caring, responsible citizens." *https://www.bgca.org/about-us/*: accessed 31 Mar 2024.

[19] The Pacific Coast Trail (PCT) (part of the National Trails System) was built with the sweat and determination of volunteers and government agencies sharing passion for a superior trail experience and the belief that building a trail from Mexico to Canada would benefit generations to come. *https://www.fs.usda.gov/pct/*: accessed 31 Mar 2024.

[20] Boys & Girls Clubs of America National Headquarters, *https://www.bgca.org/about-us/contact-us/*: accessed 31 Mar 2024.

[21] The American Board of Examiners in Clinical Social Work (ABE) is the national standard-setting organization that promotes the practice standards and issues credentials for clinical social workers. *https://www.socialworkdegreeguide.com/faq/what-is-the-american-board-of-examiners-in-clinical-social-work/*: accessed 31 Mar 2024.

[22] As a MFLC with the Mental Health Network Government Services (MHNGS) they offered behavioral health programs by licensed behavioral health practitioners who specialize in counseling family life issues including domestic violence, crisis response and post-traumatic stress. *http://www.nationalresourcedirectory.gov/resource/detail/8765448/MHN+Government+Services+Behavioral+Health+Solutions*: accessed 31 Mar 2024.

[23] Phil Cousineau, Editor, *The Hero's Journey: Joseph Campbell on His Life and Work (The Collected Works of Joseph Campbell)*, (Novato, California: New World Library, 2003).

CHAPTER FOUR: NONE OF US ARE AS GOOD, AS ALL OF US

[24] The Medal of Honor is the United States' highest award for military valor in action. And while over 150 years have passed since its inception, the meaning behind the Medal has never tarnished. Etched within are the very values that each Recipient displayed in the moments that mattered—bravery, courage, sacrifice, integrity. A deep love of country and a desire to always do what is right. "The Medal of Honor," *https://www.cmohs.org/medal*: accessed 31 Mar 2024.

[25] The Editors of Pensee, *Velikovsky Reconsidered,* New York: Doubleday Publishing, 1976. Accessed 31 Mar 2024.

[26] Jung, Carl G., John Jung, M. L. von Franz, Editors, *Man and His Symbols* (London, United Kingdom: Aldus Books Ltd., 1971), 170.

[27] LaGrave, "Honor Bound Academy" (*https://thehonorboundacademy.org/*): accessed 31 Mar 2024.

[28] It is an adaptation of a phrase by Publilius Syrus, a Latin writer of maxims (1st century BC). He wrote: Bis vincit qui se vincit in victoria meaning "He conquers twice who conquers himself when he is victorious"—control your urge to be arrogant, smug, cruel, or vindictive when you win. *https://dribbble.com /shots/5971922-Vincit-qui-se-vincit#*: accessed 1 Apr 2024.

[29] "To Benjamin Franklin from Thomas Jefferson, [21 June 1776?]," Founders Online, National Archives, https://founders.archives.gov/documents/Franklin/01–22–02–0284. [Original source: *The Papers of Benjamin Franklin,* vol. 22, March 23, 1775, through October 27, 1776, ed. William B. Willcox. New Haven and London: Yale University Press, 1982, pp. 485–486.], accessed 31 Mar 2024.

[30] Addison, II, L.C., The Tenets of Freemasonry: Mere Words or Good Guidelines? (*https://grandlodgeofiowa.org/docs/Philosophy_Masonry/TheTenetsOfFree masonry pdf*): accessed 1 Apr 2024.

[31] *Wikipedia* (*https://en.wikipedia.org/wiki/Masonic_ritual_and_symbolism*), "Masonic Ritual and Symbolism," accessed 31 Mar 2024.

[32] "Navy SEAL & RECON Special Operations Combat Medic Technician (NEC 8492)", Navy Medicine, *https://www.med.navy.mil/Navy-Medicine-Operational -Training-Command/Naval-Special-Operations-Medical-Institute/Special-Operations -Combat-Medical-Skills-Sustainment-Course/*, accessed 31 Mar 2024.

[33] Wikipedia (*https://en.wikipedia.org/wiki/Special_Warfare_insignia#:~:text =Sailors%20must%20complete%20SEAL%20Qualification,Special%20Warfare%20 (SEAL)%20Officer*) "5326 Combatant Swimmer (SEAL)" accessed 31 Mar 2024.

[34] Wikipedia (*https://en.wikipedia.org/wiki/Masonic_ritual_and_symbolism*), "Masonic Ritual and Symbolism," accessed 31 Mar 2024.

[35] Ibid.

CHAPTER SIX: ADOLESCENT COMBAT DIPLOMATE

[36] Wikipedia (*https://en.wikipedia.org/wiki/Black_Lives_Matter*) Black Lives Matter (BLM) is a decentralized political and social movement that seeks to highlight racism, discrimination, and racial inequality experienced by black people, and promote anti-racism. Accessed 1 Apr 2024.

[37] Wikipedia (*https://en.wikipedia.org/wiki/MeToo_movement*) Me Too is a social movement and awareness campaign against sexual abuse, sexual harassment,

and rape culture, in which people publicize their experiences of sexual abuse or sexual harassment. Accessed 1 Apr 2024.

[38] "Follow Your Bliss," Joseph Campbell Foundation (*https://www.jcf.org/learn /joseph-campbell-follow-your-bliss*): accessed 31 Mar 2024.

[39] Wikipedia (*https://en.wikipedia.org/wiki/Live,_Laugh,_Love*), "Live, Laugh, Love," accessed 31 Mar 2024.

[40] "Navy SEAL & RECON Special Operations Combat Medic Technician (NEC 8492)," Navy Medicine, *https://www.med.navy.mil/Navy-Medicine-Operation-al-Training-Command/Naval-Special-Operations-Medical-Institute/Special-Opera-tions-Combat-Medical-Skills-Sustainment-Course/*, accessed 31 Mar 2024.

[41] "Special Warfare Insignia," Navy Enlisted Classification (NEC) 5326 Combat-ant Swimmer (SEAL), *https://en.wikipedia.org/wiki/Special_Warfare_insignia*: accessed 31 Mar 2024.

[42] Special Operations Forces are involved in various types of missions ranging from combat and counterterrorism operations to hostage rescue and humani-tarian aid. (*https://www.military.com/special-operations*): accessed 1 Apr 2024.

CHAPTER SEVEN: WHY A MYSTERY?

[43] Ellis, David, The Psychology of Mystery (*https://www.donweaver.org/the-psychol-ogy-of-mystery/*): accessed 1 Apr 2024.

[44] Smith, Scott. "Psychology: A Sense of Mystery May Be the Spice of Life," Capi-tal Gazette, 6 Feb 2014, HTML edition (*https://www.capitalgazette.com/2014 /02/06/psychology-a-sense-of-mystery-may-be-the-spice-of-life/*) ; accessed 1 Apr 2024.

[45] The expression military–industrial complex (MIC) describes the relationship between a country's military and the defense industry that supplies it, seen together as a vested interest which influences public policy. *https://en.wikipedia. org/wiki/Military%E2%80%93industrial_complex*: accessed 1 Apr 2024.

[46] Special Operations Forces are involved in various types of missions ranging from combat and counterterrorism operations to hostage rescue and humani-tarian aid. (*https://www.military.com/special-operations*): accessed 1 Apr 2024.

[47] A private military company (PMC) or private military and security company (PMSC) is a private company providing armed combat or security services for financial gain. PMCs refer to their personnel as "security contractors" or "pri-vate military contractors". (*https://en.wikipedia.org/wiki/Private_military _company*): accessed 1 Apr 2024.

CHAPTER EIGHT: WE ARE HERE TO SERVE YOU

[48] Led Zeppelin; Songwriters—Jimmy Page, John Bonham, John Paul Jones, Robert Anthony Plant, "Good Times Bad Times," Warner Chappell Music,

Inc., 1969. *https://lyrics.lyricfind.com/lyrics/led-zeppelin-good-times-bad-times-1*: accessed 1 Apr 2024.

49 Sun Tzu was a Chinese military general, strategist, philosopher, and writer who lived during the Eastern Zhou period (771–256 BC). Sun Tzu is traditionally credited as the author of The Art of War, an influential work of military strategy that has affected both Western and East Asian philosophy and military thought. *https://en.wikipedia.org/wiki/Sun_Tzu*: accessed 1 Apr 2024.

50 Tzu, Sun, *The Art of War* (China, 5ᵗʰ Century BC (Library of Congress Class U101 .S95) *https://en.wikipedia.org/wiki/The_Art_of_War*: accessed 1 Apr 2024.

51 Griffith, Samuel B. *The Illustrated Art of War.* 2005. Oxford University Press. pp. 17, 141–43 (*https://en.wikipedia.org/wiki/The_Art_of_War*): accessed 1 Apr 2024.

52 Greatest Generation (*https://en.wikipedia.org/wiki/Greatest_Generation*) accessed 1 Apr 2024.

53 Silent Generation (*https://en.wikipedia.org/wiki/Silent_Generation*) accessed 1 Apr 2024.

54 Baby Boomers (*https://en.wikipedia.org/wiki/Baby_boomers*) accessed 1 Apr 2024.

55 Generation X (*https://en.wikipedia.org/wiki/Generation_X*) accessed 1 Apr 2024.

56 Millennials (*https://en.wikipedia.org/wiki/Millennials*) accessed 1 Apr 2024.

57 Generation Z (*https://en.wikipedia.org/wiki/Generation_Z*) accessed 1 Apr 2024.

58 Generation Alpha (*https://en.wikipedia.org/wiki/Generation_Alpha*) accessed 1 Apr 2024.

CHAPTER NINE: S.W.O.T.

59 Greatest Generation (*https://en.wikipedia.org/wiki/Greatest_Generation*) accessed 1 Apr 2024.

60 Ibid.

61 Ibid.

62 Silent Generation (*https://en.wikipedia.org/wiki/Silent_Generation*) accessed 1 Apr 2024.

63 Ibid.

64 Ibid.

65 Ibid.

66 Ibid.

67 Ibid.

68 Ibid.

69 Baby Boomers (*https://en.wikipedia.org/wiki/Baby_boomers*): accessed 21 Aug 2020.

70 Ibid.

71   Ibid.

72   Ibid.

73   Ibid.

74   Ibid.

75   Ibid.

76   *Generation X* (*https://en.wikipedia.org/wiki/Generation_X*): accessed 1 Apr 2024.

77   Ibid.

78   Ibid.

79   Ibid.

80   Ibid.

81   Ibid.

82   Ibid.

83   Pollak, Lindsey. *https://lindseypollak.com/gen-x-the-forgotten-middle-child-is-it-any* *-wonder-that-our-theme-song-is-dont-you-forget-about-me/*: accessed 2 Apr 2024.

84   Ibid.

85   Ibid.

86   *Millennials* (*https://en.wikipedia.org/wiki/Millennials*): accessed 1 Apr 2024.

87   Ibid.

88   Ibid.

89   Ibid.

90   Ibid.

91   Get Smarter with edX, The Strengths and Weaknesses of Every Generation in your Workforce (*https://www.getsmarter.com/blog/career-advice/know-your* *-generationals/*), 2 Jul 2020. Accessed 2 Apr 2024.

92   Ibid.

93   Ibid.

94   Ibid.

95   Ibid.

96   Parker, Kim and Rugh Igielnik, Pew Research Center, *On the Cusp of Adulthood and Facing an Uncertain Future: What We Know About Gen Z So Far*, 14 May 2020 (*https://www.pewresearch.org/social-trends/2020/05/14/on-the-cusp-of* *-adulthood-and-facing-an-uncertain-future-what-we-know-about-gen-z-so-far-2/*): accessed 2 Apr 2024.

97   Schleifstein, Darcy, Zachary Dougherty, and Sarah Emily Baum, *"Dear National Rifle Association: We Won't Let You Win. From, Teenagers,"* New York Times, 13 Mar 2018 (*https://www.nytimes.com/2018/03/13/opinion/nra-shooting-marjo-* *ry-stoneman-douglas.html*): accessed 2 Apr 2024.

98   Ibid.

99   Parker, Kim and Rugh Igielnik, Pew Research Center, *On the Cusp of Adulthood and Facing an Uncertain Future: What We Know About Gen Z So Far*, 14 May 2020.

100 Ibid.

CHAPTER TEN: IT BEING, AN AUTHENTIC TRUTH

[101] Julian Assange (*https://en.wikipedia.org/wiki/Julian_Assange*) accessed 2 Apr 2024.

[102] Edward Snowden (*https://en.wikipedia.org/wiki/Edward_Snowden*) accessed 2 Apr 2024.

[103] Panama Papers (*https://en.wikipedia.org/wiki/Panama_Papers*) accessed 2 Apr 2024.

[104] The ICIJ is a global network of 280 investigative journalists in more than 100 countries who collaborate on in-depth investigative stories. (*https://www.icij.org/*). Accessed 2 Apr 2024.

[105] The U.S. Department of the Treasury established several programs under TARP to help stabilize the U.S. financial system, restart economic growth, and prevent avoidable foreclosures. (*https://home.treasury.gov/data/troubled-asset-relief-program*). Accessed 2 Apr 2024.

[106] The Age of Aquarius, in astrology, is either the current or forthcoming astrological age, depending on the method of calculation. The approximate 2,160 years for each age corresponds to the average time it takes for the vernal equinox to move from one constellation of the zodiac into the next. *https://en.wikipedia.org/wiki/Age_of_Aquarius#:~:text=According%20to%20various%20astrologers'%20calculations,if%20it%20has%20already%20started.* Accessed 2 Apr 2024.

[107] Tracey B., *This is the dawning of the age of Aquarius*, posted 16 Feb 2021 (*https://thelifestyleconcept.co.uk/blog/this-is-nearly-the-dawning-of-the-age-of-aquarius/*): accessed 2 Apr 2024.

CHAPTER ELEVEN: A SOCIAL CONTRACT BROKEN

[108] LaGrave, "Honor Bound Academy" (*https://thehonorboundacademy.org/*): accessed 31 Mar 2024.

[109] Ibid.

[110] Ibid.

[111] Tolkien, J. R. R. *The Silmarillion: The legendary precursor to The Lord of the Rings*. New York, New York: Del Ray Publishing (an imprint of Penguin Random House), 2002.

[112] Ibid.

[113] LaGrave, "Honor Bound Academy" (*https://thehonorboundacademy.org/*): accessed 31 Mar 2024.

CHAPTER TWELVE: BOUND BY HONOR

[114] Epictetus Quotes. BrainyQuote.com, BrainyMedia Inc, 2024. *https://www.brainyquote.com/quotes/epictetus_106298*: accessed April 2, 2024.

[115] LaGrave, Tom, "Honor Bound Academy" (https://thehonorboundacademy. org/): accessed 31 Mar 2024.

[116] Ibid.

[117] Ibid.

[118] Ibid.

[119] Ibid.

[120] Ibid.

CHAPTER THIRTEEN: HONOR BOUND ACADEMY

[121] Ibid.

[122] Ibid.

[123] Ibid.

[124] https://www.linkedin.com/in/tjlagravejr: accessed 7 Apr 2024.

[125] Tolkien, *The Silmarillion: The legendary precursor to The Lord of the Rings.* 2002.

[126] LaGrave, Tom, "Honor Bound Academy" (https://thehonorboundacademy.org/): accessed 31 Mar 2024.

[127] https://en.wikipedia.org/wiki/Bill_Gates: accessed 7 Apr 2024.

[128] https://en.wikipedia.org/wiki/Warren_Buffett: accessed 7 Apr 2024.

[129] "Special Warfare Insignia," Navy Enlisted Classification (NEC) 5326 Combatant Swimmer (SEAL), https://en.wikipedia.org/wiki/Special_Warfare_insignia: accessed 31 Mar 2024.

[130] The Comanche is a Native American tribe from the Southern Plains of the present-day United States. Comanche people today belong to the federally recognized Comanche Nation, headquartered in Lawton, Oklahoma. https://en.wikipedia.org/wiki/Comanche: accessed 4 Jun 2020.

[131] In the fictional world of J. R. R. Tolkien, Moria, also named Khazad-dûm, is an ancient subterranean complex in Middle-earth, comprising a vast labyrinthine network of tunnels, chambers, mines and halls under the Misty Mountains, with doors on both the western and the eastern sides of the mountain range. Moria is introduced in Tolkien's novel The Hobbit, and is a major scene of action in The Lord of the Rings. https://en.wikipedia.org/wiki/Moria,_Middle-earth: accessed 21 Oct 2023.

[132] https://en.wikipedia.org/wiki/Michael_Bloomberg: accessed 7 Apr 2024.

[133] https://en.wikipedia.org/wiki/United_States_Navy_SEALs: accessed 15 Jul 2020.

[134] The Iroquois, also known as the Five Nations, and later as the Six Nations from 1722 onwards are an Iroquoian-speaking confederacy of Native Americans and First Nations peoples in northeast North America. They were known by the French during the colonial years as the Iroquois League, and later as the Iroquois Confederacy, while the English simply called them the "Five Nations".

The peoples of the Iroquois included (from east to west) the Mohawk, Oneida, Onondaga, Cayuga, and Seneca. After 1722, the Iroquoian-speaking Tuscarora people from the southeast were accepted into the confederacy, from which point it was known as the "Six Nations". *https://en.wikipedia.org/wiki/Iroquois*: accessed 16 Jun 2020.

135 In J.R.R. Tolkien's legendarium, Gondolin is a secret city of Elves in the First Age of Middle-earth, and the greatest of their cities in Beleriand. The story of the Fall of Gondolin tells of the arrival there of Tuor, a prince of Men; of the betrayal of the city to the dark Lord Morgoth by the king's nephew, Maeglin; and of its subsequent siege and catastrophic destruction by Morgoth's armies. It also relates the flight of the fugitives to the Havens of Sirion, the wedding of Tuor and the Elf Idril, and the childhood of their son Eärendil. *https://en.wikipedia.org/wiki/Gondolin*: accessed 5 Nov 2023.

136 *https://en.wikipedia.org/wiki/Larry_Ellison*: accessed 7 Apr 2024.

137 The Joint Special Operations Command (JSOC) is a joint component command of the United States Special Operations Command (USSOCOM) and is charged with studying special operations requirements and techniques to ensure interoperability and equipment standardization, to plan and conduct special operations exercises and training, to develop joint special operations tactics, and to execute special operations missions worldwide. *https://en.wikipedia.org/wiki/Joint_Special_Operations_Command*: accessed 5 Jun 2020.

138 Inuit are a group of culturally and historically similar Indigenous peoples traditionally inhabiting the Arctic and subarctic regions of North America, including Greenland, Labrador, Quebec, Nunavut, the Northwest Territories, Yukon (traditionally[a]), Alaska, and Chukotsky District of Chukotka Autonomous Okrug, Russia. *https://en.wikipedia.org/wiki/Inuit*: accessed 4 Jun 2020.

139 Minas Tirith is the capital of Gondor in J. R. R. Tolkien's fantasy novel The Lord of the Rings. It is a seven-walled fortress city built on the spur of a mountain, rising some 700 feet to a high terrace, housing the Citadel, at the seventh level. Atop this is the 300-foot high Tower of Ecthelion, which contains the throne room. *https://en.wikipedia.org/wiki/Minas_Tirith*: accessed 5 Nov 2023.

140 *https://en.wikipedia.org/wiki/Phil_Knight*: accessed 7 Apr 2024.

141 The United States Army Rangers are U.S. Army personnel who have served in any unit which has held the official designation of "Ranger". The 75th Ranger Regiment is an elite airborne light infantry combat formation within the United States Army Special Operations Command (USASOC). The Ranger Training Brigade (RTB)—headquartered at Fort Moore—is an organization under the United States Army Training and Doctrine Command (TRADOC) and is separate from the 75th Ranger Regiment. *https://en.wikipedia.org/wiki/United_States_Army_Rangers*: accessed 17 Jun 2020.

[142] The Nez Perce are an Indigenous people of the Plateau who still live on a fraction of the lands on the southeastern Columbia River Plateau in the Pacific Northwest. This region has been occupied for at least 11,500 years. *https:// en.wikipedia.org/wiki/Nez_Perce*: accessed 16 Jun 2020.

[143] Menegroth, the Thousand Caves, was the city in the land of Doriath which was home to king Thingol of the Sindarin elves and queen Melian, one of the Maiar, during the First Age. It was the location of the Menelrond, the hall where Thingol's Throne was situated. *https://tolkiengateway.net/wiki/Menegroth*: accessed 5 Nov 2023.

[144] *https://en.wikipedia.org/wiki/Elon_Musk*: accessed 7 Apr 2024.

[145] The 160th Special Operations Aviation Regiment (Airborne), abbreviated as 160th SOAR (A), is a special operations force of the United States Army that provides helicopter aviation support for special operations forces. Its missions have included attack, assault, and reconnaissance, and these missions are usually conducted at night, at high speeds, low altitudes, and on short notice. Nicknamed the Night Stalkers and called Task Force Brown within the JSOC. *https://en.wikipedia.org/wiki/160th_Special_Operations_Aviation_Regiment_(Airborne)*: accessed 5 Feb 2020.

[146] The Seminole are a Native American people who developed in Florida in the 18th century. Today, they live in Oklahoma and Florida, and comprise three federally recognized tribes: the Seminole Nation of Oklahoma, the Seminole Tribe of Florida, and the Miccosukee Tribe of Indians of Florida, as well as independent groups. *https://en.wikipedia.org/wiki/Seminole*: accessed 4 Jun 2020.

[147] In J. R. R. Tolkien's fantasy writings, Isengard is a large fortress in Nan Curunír, the Wizard's Vale, in the western part of Middle-earth. In the fantasy world, the name of the fortress is described as a translation of Angrenost, a word in the elvish language Sindarin, which Tolkien invented. *https://en.wikipedia.org/wiki/Isengard*: accessed 5 Nov 2023.

[148] *https://en.wikipedia.org/wiki/Jeff_Bezos*: accessed 7 Apr 2024.

[149] The United States Army Special Forces (SF), colloquially known as the "Green Berets" due to their distinctive service headgear, are a special operations force of the United States Army. *https://en.wikipedia.org/wiki/United_States_Army_Special_Forces*: accessed 17 Jun 2020.

[150] The Navajo are a Native American people of the Southwestern United States the Navajo Nation is the largest federally recognized tribe in the United States; additionally, the Navajo Nation has the largest reservation in the country. *https://en.wikipedia.org/wiki/Navajo*: accessed 4 Jun 2020.

[151] Rivendell (Sindarin: Imladris) is a valley in J. R. R. Tolkien's fictional world of Middle-earth, representing both a homely place of sanctuary and a magical Elvish otherworld. It is an important location in The Hobbit and The Lord

of the Rings, being the place where the quest to destroy the One Ring began. *https://en.wikipedia.org/wiki/Rivendell*: accessed 1 Apr 2024.

[152] *https://en.wikipedia.org/wiki/Carl_Icahn*: accessed 7 Apr 2024.

[153] United States Marine Forces Special Operations Command (MARSOC) is a component command of the United States Special Operations Command (SOCOM) that comprises the Marine Corps' contribution to SOCOM. Its core capabilities are direct action, special reconnaissance and foreign internal defense. MARSOC has also been directed to conduct counter-terrorism and information operations. *https://en.wikipedia.org/wiki/United_States_Marine _Forces_Special_Operations_Command*: accessed 10 Aug 2020.

[154] The Cherokee Nation formerly known as the Cherokee Nation of Oklahoma, is the largest of three federally recognized tribes of Cherokees in the United States. It includes people descended from members of the Old Cherokee Nation who relocated, due to increasing pressure, from the Southeast to Indian Territory and Cherokees who were forced to relocate on the Trail of Tears. *https://en .wikipedia.org/wiki/Cherokee_Nation*: accessed 11 Aug 2020.

[155] Belegost was one of two great Dwarven cities in the Blue Mountains, the other being Nogrod. It was home to the Dwarves of Belegost. Belegost was in the north central part of the Blue Mountains, northeast of Mount Dolmed, north of Nogrod, and not far from lake Nenuial guarding one of the only passes over the Blue Mountains. *https://tolkiengateway.net/wiki/Belegost*: accessed 7 Apr 2024.

[156] *https://en.wikipedia.org/wiki/Mark_Zuckerberg*: accessed 7 Apr 2024.

[157] Pararescuemen (also known as PJs) are United States Air Force airmen who conduct personnel recovery and combat search and rescue operations as well as other missions for the U.S. military and its allies. Highly trained special operators, PJs are generally assigned to Air Force Special Operations Command (AFSOC) and Air Combat Command (ACC). *https://en.wikipedia.org/wiki /United_States_Air_Force_Pararescue*: accessed 17 Jun 2020.

[158] The Lakota are a Native American people. Also known as the Teton Sioux (from Thítȟuŋwaŋ), they are one of the three prominent subcultures of the Sioux people, with the Eastern Dakota (Santee) and Western Dakota (Wičhíyena). Their current lands are in North and South Dakota. *https:// en.wikipedia.org/wiki/Lakota_people*: accessed 7 Apr 2024.

[159] Nogrod, also known as Tumunzahar by the Eldar and Hollowbold by the Edain, was one of seven of the Ancient Mansions of the Dwarf Fathers. Its people were thought to be known as the Firebeards, with the Broadbeams residing in Belegost. It was located in the BlueMountains just to south-west of Belegost and was famed for its craftsmen, whose renown for fashioning the finest steel, weapons and mail was legendary. Chief among these was Telchar and his master Gamil Zirak the Old. *http://thetolkienwiki.org/wiki.cgi?Nogrod*: accessed 1 Apr 2023.

[160] *https://en.wikipedia.org/wiki/Larry_Page*: accessed 7 Apr 2024.

[161] The United States Air Force Combat Control Teams, singular Combat Controller (CCT) (AFSC 1Z2X1), are an elite special operations force (specifically known as "special tactics operators") who specialize in all aspects of air-ground communication, as well as air traffic control, fire support (including rotary and fixed-wing close air support), and command, control, and communications in covert, forward, or austere environments. *https://en.wikipedia.org/wiki/United _States_Air_Force_Combat_Control_Team*: accessed 5 Jun 2020.

[162] The Grand Traverse Band of Ottawa and Chippewa Indians is a federally recognized Native American tribe located in northwest Michigan on the Leelanau Peninsula. *https://en.wikipedia.org/wiki/Grand_Traverse_Band_of_Ottawa_and _Chippewa_Indians*: accessed 4 Jun 2020.

[163] Nargothrond was spread over miles and miles of tunnels and caves made out of rock in multiple different shapes and sizes. The rock used was most probably limestone. Right in the center of those caves and tunnels were three Great Halls in which the king of the city used to sit. A deep-seated chamber stood deep into the cave where Glaurung hid the remnants of the Nargothrond treasures and sat upon it until his departure. *https://thetolkien.forum/wiki/Nargothrond*: accessed 1 Apr 2024.

[164] *https://en.wikipedia.org/wiki/Sergey_Brin*: accessed 7 Apr 2024.

[165] Special Reconnaissance (SR), formerly Special Operations Weather Technician or Team (SOWT), is conducted by trained Air Force personnel assigned to Special Tactics Squadrons of the United States Air Force Special Operations Command who operate deep behind enemy lines to conduct covert direction of air and missile attacks, place remotely monitored sensors, and support other special operation units. *https://en.wikipedia.org/wiki/United_States_Air_Force _Special_Reconnaissance*: accessed21 Oct 2023.

[166] The Natchez are a Native American people who originally lived in the Natchez Bluffs area in the Lower Mississippi Valley, near the present-day city of Natchez, Mississippi, in the United States. *https://en.wikipedia.org/wiki/Natchez _people*: accessed 4 Jun 2020.

[167] The Grey Havens, also known as Mithlond, were seaports on both sides of the end of the Gulf of Lune near the mouth of the River Lhûn in western Eriador. Founded by the Elves of Lindon in S.A.1 the Grey Havens were known for their good harbourage and many ships; these were used by any of the Eldar to leave Middle-earth for Eressëa or Valinor. Círdan was Lord of the Havens from its foundation and into the Fourth Age. *https://tolkiengateway.net/wiki/Grey _Havens*: accessed 7 Apr 2024.

[168] "Special Warfare Insignia," Navy Enlisted Classification (NEC) 5326 Combatant Swimmer (SEAL), *https://en.wikipedia.org/wiki/Special_Warfare_insignia*: accessed 31 Mar 2024.

169 LaGrave, Tom, *"Honor Bound Academy"* (*https://thehonorboundacademy.org/*): accessed 31 Mar 2024.

170 *https://en.wikipedia.org/wiki/Moria,_Middle-earth*: accessed 21 Oct 2023.

171 *https://en.wikipedia.org/wiki/Comanche*: accessed 4 Jun 2020.

172 *https://en.wikipedia.org/wiki/Moria,_Middle-earth*: accessed 21 Oct 2023.

173 *https://en.wikipedia.org/wiki/Bill_Gates*: accessed 7 Apr 2024.

174 *https://en.wikipedia.org/wiki/Warren_Buffett*: accessed 7 Apr 2024.

175 "Special Warfare Insignia," Navy Enlisted Classification (NEC) 5326 Combatant Swimmer (SEAL), *https://en.wikipedia.org/wiki/Special_Warfare_insignia*: accessed 31 Mar 2024.

176 *https://en.wikipedia.org/wiki/Comanche*: accessed 4 Jun 2020.

177 *https://en.wikipedia.org/wiki/Moria,_Middle-earth*: accessed 21 Oct 2023.

178 *https://en.wikipedia.org/wiki/Moria,_Middle-earth*: accessed 21 Oct 2023.

179 Ibid.

180 Ibid.

181 Ibid.

182 Ibid.

183 LaGrave, Tom, "Honor Bound Academy" (*https://thehonorboundacademy.org/*): accessed 31 Mar 2024.

184 LaGrave, Tom, "Honor Bound Academy" (*https://thehonorboundacademy.org/*): accessed 31 Mar 2024.

185 https://en.wikipedia.org/wiki/Moria,_Middle-earth: accessed 21 Oct 2023.

186 LaGrave, Tom, "Honor Bound Academy" (*https://thehonorboundacademy.org/*): accessed 31 Mar 2024.

187 Tolkien, *The Silmarillion: The legendary precursor to The Lord of the Rings.* 2002.

188 LaGrave, Tom, "Honor Bound Academy" (*https://thehonorboundacademy.org/*): accessed 31 Mar 2024.

189 *https://en.wikipedia.org/wiki/Moria,_Middle-earth*: accessed 21 Oct 2023.

190 LaGrave, Tom, "Honor Bound Academy" (*https://thehonorboundacademy.org/*): accessed 31 Mar 2024.

191 *https://en.wikipedia.org/wiki/Moria,_Middle-earth*: accessed 21 Oct 2023.

192 Ibid.

193 Ibid.

194 Ibid.

195 Ibid.

196 *https://en.wikipedia.org/wiki/Moria,_Middle-earth*: accessed 21 Oct 2023.

197 LaGrave, Tom, "Honor Bound Academy" (*https://thehonorboundacademy.org/*): accessed 31 Mar 2024.

198 LaGrave, Tom, "Honor Bound Academy" (*https://thehonorboundacademy.org/*): accessed 31 Mar 2024.

[199] *https://en.wikipedia.org/wiki/Moria,_Middle-earth*: accessed 21 Oct 2023.

[200] LaGrave, Tom, "Honor Bound Academy" (*https://thehonorboundacademy.org/*): accessed 31 Mar 2024.

[201] *https://en.wikipedia.org/wiki/Moria,_Middle-earth*: accessed 21 Oct 2023.

[202] *https://en.wikipedia.org/wiki/Bill_Gates*: accessed 7 Apr 2024.

[203] *https://en.wikipedia.org/wiki/Warren_Buffett*: accessed 7 Apr 2024.

[204] "Special Warfare Insignia," Navy Enlisted Classification (NEC) 5326 Combatant Swimmer (SEAL), *https://en.wikipedia.org/wiki/Special_Warfare_insignia*: accessed 31 Mar 2024.

[205] *https://en.wikipedia.org/wiki/Comanche*: accessed 4 Jun 2020.

[206] *https://en.wikipedia.org/wiki/Moria,_Middle-earth*: accessed 21 Oct 2023.

[207] LaGrave, Tom, "Honor Bound Academy" (*https://thehonorboundacademy.org/*): accessed 31 Mar 2024.

[208] Ibid.

[209] LaGrave, Tom, "Honor Bound Academy" (*https://thehonorboundacademy.org/*): accessed 31 Mar 2024.

[210] *https://en.wikipedia.org/wiki/Gondolin*: accessed 5 Nov 2023.

[211] *https://en.wikipedia.org/wiki/Michael_Bloomberg*: accessed 7 Apr 2024.

[212] *https://en.wikipedia.org/wiki/United_States_Navy_SEALs*: accessed 15 Jul 2020.

[213] *https://en.wikipedia.org/wiki/Iroquois*: accessed 16 Jun 2020.

[214] *https://en.wikipedia.org/wiki/Gondolin*: accessed 5 Nov 2023.

[215] LaGrave, Tom, "Honor Bound Academy" (*https://thehonorboundacademy.org*): accessed 31 Mar 2024.

[216] *https://en.wikipedia.org/wiki/Moria,_Middle-earth*: accessed 21 Oct 2023.

[217] LaGrave, Tom, "Honor Bound Academy" (*https://thehonorboundacademy.org/*): accessed 31 Mar 2024.

[218] *https://en.wikipedia.org/wiki/Gondolin*: accessed 5 Nov 2023.

[219] LaGrave, Tom, "Honor Bound Academy" (*https://thehonorboundacademy.org/*): accessed 31 Mar 2024.

[220] *https://en.wikipedia.org/wiki/Gondolin*: accessed 5 Nov 2023 .

[221] Tolkien, *The Silmarillion: The legendary precursor to The Lord of the Rings.* 2002.

[222] *https://en.wikipedia.org/wiki/Gondolin*: accessed 5 Nov 2023.

[223] Ibid.

[224] Ibid.

[225] Ibid.

[226] Ibid.

[227] Ibid.

[228] LaGrave, Tom, "Honor Bound Academy" (*https://thehonorboundacademy.org/*): accessed 31 Mar 2024.

[229] *https://en.wikipedia.org/wiki/Gondolin*: accessed 5 Nov 2023.

230 *https://en.wikipedia.org/wiki/Iroquois*: accessed 16 Jun 2020.

231 *https://en.wikipedia.org/wiki/Gondolin*: accessed 5 Nov 2023.

232 Ibid.

233 *https://en.wikipedia.org/wiki/Iroquois*: accessed 16 Jun 2020.

234 LaGrave, Tom, "Honor Bound Academy" (*https://thehonorboundacademy.org/*): accessed 31 Mar 2024.

235 Ibid.

236 Ibid.

237 *https://en.wikipedia.org/wiki/Minas_Tirith*: accessed 5 Nov 2023.

238 *https://en.wikipedia.org/wiki/Larry_Ellison*: accessed 7 Apr 2024.

239 *https://en.wikipedia.org/wiki/Joint_Special_Operations_Command*: accessed 5 Jun 2020.

240 *https://en.wikipedia.org/wiki/Inuit*: accessed 4 Jun 2020.

241 *https://en.wikipedia.org/wiki/Minas_Tirith*: accessed 5 Nov 2023.

242 LaGrave, Tom, "Honor Bound Academy" (*https://thehonorboundacademy.org/*): accessed 31 Mar 2024.

243 *https://en.wikipedia.org/wiki/Minas_Tirith*: accessed 5 Nov 2023.

244 Ibid.

245 Ibid.

246 LaGrave, Tom, "Honor Bound Academy" (*https://thehonorboundacademy.org/*): accessed 31 Mar 2024.

247 *https://en.wikipedia.org/wiki/Larry_Ellison*: accessed 7 Apr 2024.

248 LaGrave, Tom, "Honor Bound Academy" (*https://thehonorboundacademy.org/*): accessed 31 Mar 2024.

249 *https://en.wikipedia.org/wiki/Inuit*: accessed 4 Jun 2020.

250 *https://en.wikipedia.org/wiki/Joint_Special_Operations_Command*: accessed 5 Jun 2020.

251 *https://en.wikipedia.org/wiki/Inuit*: accessed 4 Jun 2020.

252 Ibid.

253 Ibid.

254 Ibid.

255 Ibid.

256 Ibid.

257 *https://en.wikipedia.org/wiki/Joint_Special_Operations_Command*: accessed 5 Jun 2020.

258 *https://en.wikipedia.org/wiki/Joint_Special_Operations_Command*: accessed 5 Jun 2020.

259 *https://en.wikipedia.org/wiki/Minas_Tirith*: accessed 5 Nov 2023.

260 LaGrave, Tom, "Honor Bound Academy" (*https://thehonorboundacademy.org/*): accessed 31 Mar 2024.

[261] *https://en.wikipedia.org/wiki/Joint_Special_Operations_Command*: accessed 5 Jun 2020.

[262] Ibid.

[263] Ibid.

[264] LaGrave, Tom, "Honor Bound Academy" (*https://thehonorboundacademy.org/*): accessed 31 Mar 2024.

[265] *https://en.wikipedia.org/wiki/Minas_Tirith*: accessed 5 Nov 2023.

[266] *https://en.wikipedia.org/wiki/Joint_Special_Operations_Command*: accessed 5 Jun 2020.

[267] *https://en.wikipedia.org/wiki/Minas_Tirith*: accessed 5 Nov 2023.

[268] *https://www.linkedin.com/in/tjlagravejr*: accessed 7 Apr 2024.

[269] *https://tolkiengateway.net/wiki/Menegroth*: accessed 5 Nov 2023.

[270] *https://en.wikipedia.org/wiki/Phil_Knight*: accessed 7 Apr 2024.

[271] *https://en.wikipedia.org/wiki/United_States_Army_Rangers*: accessed 17 Jun 2020.

[272] *https://en.wikipedia.org/wiki/Nez_Perce*: accessed 16 Jun 2020.

[273] *https://tolkiengateway.net/wiki/Menegroth*: accessed 5 Nov 2023.

[274] LaGrave, Tom, "Honor Bound Academy" (*https://thehonorboundacademy.org/*): accessed 31 Mar 2024.

[275] *https://tolkiengateway.net/wiki/Menegroth*: accessed 5 Nov 2023.

[276] *https://en.wikipedia.org/wiki/Moria,_Middle-earth*: accessed 21 Oct 2023.

[277] *https://tolkiengateway.net/wiki/Menegroth*: accessed 5 Nov 2023.

[278] Ibid.

[279] *https://en.wikipedia.org/wiki/Phil_Knight*: accessed 7 Apr 2024.

[280] *https://en.wikipedia.org/wiki/Nez_Perce*: accessed 16 Jun 2020.

[281] Ibid.

[282] Ibid.

[283] *https://www.linkedin.com/pulse/adolescent-combat-diplomate-tom-la-grave-6c?trk=articles_directory*: accessed 8 Apr 2024.

[284] *https://en.wikipedia.org/wiki/Phil_Knight*: accessed 7 Apr 2024.

[285] *https://en.wikipedia.org/wiki/Nez_Perce*: accessed 16 Jun 2020.

[286] *https://tolkiengateway.net/wiki/Menegroth*: accessed 5 Nov 2023.

[287] *https://en.wikipedia.org/wiki/United_States_Army_Rangers*: accessed 17 Jun 2020.

[288] Ibid.

[289] Ibid.

[290] Ibid.

[291] Ibid.

[292] *https://en.wikipedia.org/wiki/Moria,_Middle-earth*: accessed 21 Oct 2023.

[293] *https://en.wikipedia.org/wiki/Gondolin*: accessed 5 Nov 2023.

294 LaGrave, Tom, "Honor Bound Academy" (*https://thehonorboundacademy.org/*): accessed 31 Mar 2024.

295 *https://tolkiengateway.net/wiki/Menegroth*: accessed 5 Nov 2023.

296 LaGrave, Tom, "Honor Bound Academy" (*https://thehonorboundacademy.org*): accessed 31 Mar 2024.

297 *https://en.wikipedia.org/wiki/Isengard*: accessed 5 Nov 2023.

298 https://en.wikipedia.org/wiki/Elon_Musk: accessed 7 Apr 2024.

299 *https://en.wikipedia.org/wiki/160th_Special_Operations_Aviation_Regiment _(Airborne)*: accessed 5 Feb 2020.

300 *https://en.wikipedia.org/wiki/Seminole*: accessed 4 Jun 2020.

301 *https://en.wikipedia.org/wiki/Isengard*: accessed 5 Nov 2023.

302 LaGrave, Tom, "Honor Bound Academy" (*https://thehonorboundacademy.org/*): accessed 31 Mar 2024.

303 *https://en.wikipedia.org/wiki/Isengard*: accessed 5 Nov 2023.

304 Ibid.

305 Ibid.

306 Ibid.

307 Ibid.

308 *https://en.wikipedia.org/wiki/Elon_Musk*: accessed 7 Apr 2024.

309 LaGrave, Tom, "Honor Bound Academy" (*https://thehonorboundacademy.org/*): accessed 31 Mar 2024.

310 Ibid.

311 *https://en.wikipedia.org/wiki/Elon_Musk*: accessed 7 Apr 2024.

312 *https://en.wikipedia.org/wiki/Isengard*: accessed 5 Nov 2023.

313 *https://en.wikipedia.org/wiki/Elon_Musk*: accessed 7 Apr 2024.

314 *https://en.wikipedia.org/wiki/Seminole*: accessed 4 Jun 2020.

315 Ibid.

316 Ibid.

317 Ibid.

318 Ibid.

319 Operation Eagle Claw was a failed operation by the United States Armed Forces ordered by U.S. President Jimmy Carter to attempt the rescue of 52 embassy staff held captive at the Embassy of the United States, Tehran on 24 April 1980. *https://en.wikipedia.org/wiki/Operation_Eagle_Claw*: accessed 8 Apr 2024.

320 *https://en.wikipedia.org/wiki/160th_Special_Operations_Aviation_Regiment _(Airborne)*: accessed 5 Feb 2020.

321 Ibid.

322 Ibid.

323 Ibid.

[324] LaGrave, Tom, "Honor Bound Academy" (*https://thehonorboundacademy.org/*): accessed 31 Mar 2024.

[325] https://en.wikipedia.org/wiki/Isengard: accessed 5 Nov 2023.

[326] https://en.wikipedia.org/wiki/Elon_Musk: accessed 7 Apr 2024.

[327] *https://en.wikipedia.org/wiki/Seminole*: accessed 4 Jun 2020.

[328] Ibid.

[329] *https://en.wikipedia.org/wiki/160th_Special_Operations_Aviation_Regiment_(Airborne)*: accessed 5 Feb 2020.

[330] *https://en.wikipedia.org/wiki/Rivendell*: accessed 1 Apr 2024.

[331] *https://en.wikipedia.org/wiki/Jeff_Bezos*: accessed 7 Apr 2024.

[332] *https://en.wikipedia.org/wiki/United_States_Army_Special_Forces*: accessed 17 Jun 2020.

[333] *https://en.wikipedia.org/wiki/Navajo*: accessed 4 Jun 2020.

[334] *https://en.wikipedia.org/wiki/Rivendell*: accessed 1 Apr 2024.

[335] LaGrave, Tom, "Honor Bound Academy" (*https://thehonorboundacademy.org/*): accessed 31 Mar 2024.

[336] *https://en.wikipedia.org/wiki/Rivendell*: accessed 1 Apr 2024.

[337] Ibid.

[338] In Irish mythology, Tír na nÓg or Tír na hÓige ('Land of Youth') is one of the names for the Celtic Otherworld, or perhaps for a part of it. Tír na nÓg is best known from the tale of Oisín and Niamh. *https://en.wikipedia.org/wiki/T%C3%ADr_na_n%C3%93g#:~:text=In%20Irish%20mythology%2C%20T%C3%ADr%20na,tale%20of%20Ois%C3%ADn%20and%20Niamh*. Accessed 8 Apr 2024.

[339] *https://en.wikipedia.org/wiki/Rivendell*: accessed 1 Apr 2024.

[340] LaGrave, Tom, "Honor Bound Academy" (*https://thehonorboundacademy.org/*): accessed 31 Mar 2024.

[341] *https://en.wikipedia.org/wiki/Rivendell*: accessed 1 Apr 2024.

[342] Ibid.

[343] *https://en.wikipedia.org/wiki/New_Mexico*: accessed 8 Apr 2024.

[344] Ibid.

[345] *https://en.wikipedia.org/wiki/Rivendell*: accessed 1 Apr 2024.

[346] *https://en.wikipedia.org/wiki/Jeff_Bezos*: accessed 7 Apr 2024.

[347] *https://www.washingtonpost.com/*: accessed 8 Apr 2024.

[348] *https://en.wikipedia.org/wiki/Jeff_Bezos*: accessed 7 Apr 2024.

[349] Ibid.

[350] *https://en.wikipedia.org/wiki/Navajo*: accessed 4 Jun 2020.

[351] LaGrave, Tom, "Honor Bound Academy" (*https://thehonorboundacademy.org/*): accessed 31 Mar 2024.

[352] *https://en.wikipedia.org/wiki/New_Mexico*: accessed 8 Apr 2024.

[353] *https://en.wikipedia.org/wiki/Navajo*: accessed 4 Jun 2020.

[354] Ibid.

[355] Ibid.

[356] Ibid.

[357] *Walk in beauty is the translation of the Navajo term for the spiritual path of celebrating the sacredness of life. https://www.walk-in-beauty.org/*: accessed 8 Apr 2024.

[358] *https://en.wikipedia.org/wiki/Navajo*: accessed 4 Jun 2020.

[359] Ibid.

[360] *https://en.wikipedia.org/wiki/United_States_Army_Special_Forces*: accessed 17 Jun 2020.

[361] *https://en.wikipedia.org/wiki/Jeff_Bezos*: accessed 7 Apr 2024.

[362] *https://en.wikipedia.org/wiki/Rivendell*: accessed 1 Apr 2024.

[363] *https://en.wikipedia.org/wiki/United_States_Army_Special_Forces*: accessed 17 Jun 2020.

[364] Ibid.

[365] Ibid.

[366] Ibid.

[367] *https://en.wikipedia.org/wiki/Rivendell*: accessed 1 Apr 2024.

[368] *https://en.wikipedia.org/wiki/Jeff_Bezos*: accessed 7 Apr 2024.

[369] *https://en.wikipedia.org/wiki/Navajo*: accessed 4 Jun 2020.

[370] *https://en.wikipedia.org/wiki/United_States_Army_Special_Forces*: accessed 17 Jun 2020.

[371] *https://tolkiengateway.net/wiki/Belegost*: accessed 7 Apr 2024.

[372] *https://en.wikipedia.org/wiki/Carl_Icahn*: accessed 7 Apr 2024.

[373] *https://en.wikipedia.org/wiki/United_States_Marine_Forces_Special_Operations_Command*: accessed 10 Aug 2020.

[374] *https://en.wikipedia.org/wiki/Cherokee_Nation*: accessed 11 Aug 2020.

[375] *https://tolkiengateway.net/wiki/Belegost*: accessed 7 Apr 2024.

[376] LaGrave, Tom, "Honor Bound Academy" (*https://thehonorboundacademy.org/*): accessed 31 Mar 2024.

[377] *https://tolkiengateway.net/wiki/Belegost*: accessed 7 Apr 2024.

[378] Ibid.

[379] Ibid.

[380] Ibid.

[381] Ibid.

[382] Ibid.

[383] Ibid.

[384] Ibid.

[385] *https://tolkiengateway.net/wiki/Menegroth*: accessed 5 Nov 2023.

[386] Tolkien, *The Silmarillion: The legendary precursor to The Lord of the Rings*. 2002.

[387] LaGrave, Tom, "Honor Bound Academy" (*https://thehonorboundacademy.org/*): accessed 31 Mar 2024.

[388] Ibid.

[389] *https://tolkiengateway.net/wiki/Belegost*: accessed 7 Apr 2024.

[390] *https://en.wikipedia.org/wiki/Carl_Icahn*: accessed 7 Apr 2024.

[391] Ibid.

[392] Ibid.

[393] Ibid.

[394] "Ruthless." *Merriam-Webster.com Dictionary, Merriam-Webster, https://www.merriam-webster.com/dictionary/ruthless* . Accessed 8 Apr. 2024.

[395] *https://en.wikipedia.org/wiki/Carl_Icahn*: accessed 7 Apr 2024.

[396] *https://tolkiengateway.net/wiki/Belegost*: accessed 7 Apr 2024.

[397] *https://en.wikipedia.org/wiki/Cherokee_Nation*: accessed 11 Aug 2020.

[398] Ibid.

[399] *https://en.wikipedia.org/wiki/Carl_Icahn*: accessed 7 Apr 2024.

[400] *https://en.wikipedia.org/wiki/United_States_Marine_Forces_Special_Operations_Command*: accessed 10 Aug 2020.

[401] Ibid.

[402] Ibid.

[403] Ibid.

[404] Ibid.

[405] "Special Warfare Insignia," Navy Enlisted Classification (NEC) 5326 Combatant Swimmer (SEAL), *https://en.wikipedia.org/wiki/Special_Warfare_insignia*: accessed 31 Mar 2024.

[406] LaGrave, Tom, "Honor Bound Academy" (*https://thehonorboundacademy.org/*): accessed 31 Mar 2024.

[407] *https://en.wikipedia.org/wiki/Carl_Icahn*: accessed 7 Apr 2024.

[408] *https://en.wikipedia.org/wiki/United_States_Marine_Forces_Special_Operations_Command*: accessed 10 Aug 2020.

[409] *http://thetolkienwiki.org/wiki.cgi?Nogrod*: accessed 1 Apr 2023.

[410] *https://en.wikipedia.org/wiki/Mark_Zuckerberg*: accessed 7 Apr 2024.

[411] *https://en.wikipedia.org/wiki/United_States_Air_Force_Pararescue*: accessed 17 Jun 2020.

[412] *https://en.wikipedia.org/wiki/Lakota_people*: accessed 7 Apr 2024.

[413] *http://thetolkienwiki.org/wiki.cgi?Nogrod*: accessed 1 Apr 2023.

[414] *https://tolkiengateway.net/wiki/Belegost*: accessed 7 Apr 2024.

[415] LaGrave, Tom, "Honor Bound Academy" (*https://thehonorboundacademy.org/*): accessed 31 Mar 2024.

[416] *http://thetolkienwiki.org/wiki.cgi?Nogrod*: accessed 1 Apr 2023.

[417] Tolkien, *The Silmarillion: The legendary precursor to The Lord of the Rings.* 2002.

[418] *http://thetolkienwiki.org/wiki.cgi?Nogrod*: accessed 1 Apr 2023.

[419] Ibid.

[420] Ibid.

[421] Ibid.

[422] *https://en.wikipedia.org/wiki/Mark_Zuckerberg*: accessed 7 Apr 2024.

[423] Ibid.

[424] Ibid.

[425] Ibid.

[426] Ibid.

[427] Ibid.

[428] LaGrave, Tom, "Honor Bound Academy" (*https://thehonorboundacademy.org/*): accessed 31 Mar 2024.

[429] *https://en.wikipedia.org/wiki/Mark_Zuckerberg*: accessed 7 Apr 2024.

[430] *https://en.wikipedia.org/wiki/Lakota_people*: accessed 7 Apr 2024.

[431] Ibid.

[432] *https://www.linkedin.com/pulse/adolescent-combat-diplomate-tom-lagrave -1e?trk=pulse-article_more-articles_related-content-card*: accessed 8 Apr 2024.

[433] *https://en.wikipedia.org/wiki/Mark_Zuckerberg*: accessed 7 Apr 2024.

[434] Ibid.

[435] *http://thetolkienwiki.org/wiki.cgi?Nogrod*: accessed 1 Apr 2023.

[436] *https://en.wikipedia.org/wiki/Lakota_people*: accessed 7 Apr 2024.

[437] *https://en.wikipedia.org/wiki/United_States_Air_Force_Pararescue*: accessed 17 Jun 2020.

[438] Ibid.

[439] *https://en.wikipedia.org/wiki/Lakota_people*: accessed 7 Apr 2024.

[440] *https://en.wikipedia.org/wiki/United_States_Air_Force_Pararescue*: accessed 17 Jun 2020.

[441] *https://www.doctrine.af.mil/Portals/61/documents/AFDP_3-50/3-50-AFDP -Personnel-Recovery.pdf*, p. 2: accessed 8 Apr 2024.

[442] *https://thetolkien.forum/wiki/Nargothrond*: accessed 1 Apr 2024.

[443] *https://en.wikipedia.org/wiki/Larry_Page*: accessed 7 Apr 2024.

[444] *https://en.wikipedia.org/wiki/United_States_Air_Force_Combat_Control _Team*: accessed 5 Jun 2020.

[445] *https://en.wikipedia.org/wiki/Grand_Traverse_Band_of_Ottawa_and_Chippewa _Indians*: accessed 4 Jun 2020.

[446] *https://thetolkien.forum/wiki/Nargothrond*: accessed 1 Apr 2024.

[447] LaGrave, Tom, "Honor Bound Academy" (*https://thehonorboundacademy.org/*): accessed 31 Mar 2024.

[448] *https://tolkiengateway.net/wiki/Menegroth*: accessed 5 Nov 2023.

[449] *https://thetolkien.forum/wiki/Nargothrond*: accessed 1 Apr 2024.

[450] *https://en.wikipedia.org/wiki/Gondolin*: accessed 5 Nov 2023.

[451] Tolkien, *The Silmarillion: The legendary precursor to The Lord of the Rings.* 2002.

[452] LaGrave, Tom, "Honor Bound Academy" (*https://thehonorboundacademy.org/*): accessed 31 Mar 2024.

[453] *https://www.linkedin.com/pulse/adolescent-combat-diplomate-tom-lagrave-9c*: accessed 9 Apr 2024.

[454] *https://en.wikipedia.org/wiki/Larry_Page*: accessed 7 Apr 2024.

[455] Ibid.

[456] Ibid.

[457] Ibid.

[458] Ibid.

[459] Ibid.

[460] *https://en.wikipedia.org/wiki/Grand_Traverse_Band_of_Ottawa_and_Chippewa _Indians*: accessed 4 Jun 2020.

[461] Ibid.

[462] LaGrave, Tom, "Honor Bound Academy" (*https://thehonorboundacademy.org/*): accessed 31 Mar 2024.

[463] *The Lamentation of the Overflowing Heart of the Red Man of the Forest. http:// www.nanations.com/ottawachippewa/lamentation.htm*: accessed 9 Apr 2024.

[464] Ibid.

[465] *https://en.wikipedia.org/wiki/United_States_Air_Force_Combat_Control_Team*: accessed 5 Jun 2020.

[466] Ibid.

[467] LaGrave, Tom, "Honor Bound Academy" (*https://thehonorboundacademy.org/*): accessed 31 Mar 2024.

[468] *https://en.wikipedia.org/wiki/United_States_Air_Force_Combat_Control_Team*: accessed 5 Jun 2020.

[469] Ibid.

[470] Ibid.

[471] *https://en.wikipedia.org/wiki/Larry_Page*: accessed 7 Apr 2024.

[472] *https://en.wikipedia.org/wiki/Grand_Traverse_Band_of_Ottawa_and_Chippewa _Indians*: accessed 4 Jun 2020.

[473] *The Twenty-one Precepts or Moral Commandments of the Ottawa and Chippewa Indians. https://www.nanations.com/ottawachippewa/twenty-oneprecepts.htm*: accessed 9 April 2024.

[474] *https://en.wikipedia.org/wiki/United_States_Air_Force_Combat_Control_Team*: accessed 5 Jun 2020.

[475] *https://tolkiengateway.net/wiki/Grey_Havens*: accessed 7 Apr 2024.

[476] *https://en.wikipedia.org/wiki/Sergey_Brin*: accessed 7 Apr 2024.

[477] *https://en.wikipedia.org/wiki/United_States_Air_Force_Special_Reconnaissance*: accessed 21 Oct 2023.

[478] *https://en.wikipedia.org/wiki/Natchez_people*: accessed 4 Jun 2020.

[479] *https://tolkiengateway.net/wiki/Grey_Havens*: accessed 7 Apr 2024.

[480] LaGrave, Tom, "Honor Bound Academy" (*https://thehonorboundacademy.org/*): accessed 31 Mar 2024.

[481] *https://www.linkedin.com/pulse/adolescent-combat-diplomate-tom-la-grave-6c?trk=articles_directory*: accessed 8 Apr 2024.

[482] Tolkien, *The Silmarillion: The legendary precursor to The Lord of the Rings*. 2002.

[483] *https://tolkiengateway.net/wiki/Grey_Havens*: accessed 7 Apr 2024.

[484] *Lotr—The Gray Havens—Watchtower. https://ideas.lego.com/projects.* (excerpt from *http://lotr.wikia.com*): accessed 9 Apr 2024.

[485] *https://tolkiengateway.net/wiki/Grey_Havens*: accessed 7 Apr 2024.

[486] Ibid.

[487] Ibid.

[488] *https://en.wikipedia.org/wiki/Sergey_Brin*: accessed 7 Apr 2024.

[489] LaGrave, Tom, "Honor Bound Academy" (*https://thehonorboundacademy.org /*): accessed 31 Mar 2024.

[490] *https://en.wikipedia.org/wiki/Larry_Page*: accessed 7 Apr 2024.

[491] *https://thetolkien.forum/wiki/Nargothrond*: accessed 1 Apr 2024.

[492] LaGrave, Tom, "Honor Bound Academy" (*https://thehonorboundacademy.org/*): accessed 31 Mar 2024.

[493] *https://tolkiengateway.net/wiki/Grey_Havens*: accessed 7 Apr 2024.

[494] *https://en.wikipedia.org/wiki/Sergey_Brin*: accessed 7 Apr 2024.

[495] *https://en.wikipedia.org/wiki/Natchez_people*: accessed 4 Jun 2020.

[496] Ibid.

[497] Ibid.

[498] Ibid.

[499] *https://en.wikipedia.org/wiki/United_States_Air_Force_Special_Reconnaissance*: accessed 21 Oct 2023.

[500] Ibid.

[501] Ibid.

[502] LaGrave, Tom, "Honor Bound Academy" (*https://thehonorboundacademy.org/*): accessed 31 Mar 2024.

[503] Ibid.

[504] Ibid.

[505] Ibid.

www.ingramcontent.com/pod-product-compliance
Lightning Source LLC
Chambersburg PA
CBHW070804280326
41934CB00012B/3051